HAWAII'S PEOPLE

UNIVERSITY OF HAWAII PRESS

Honolulu, Hawaii, 1967

third edition

HAWAII'S PEOPLE

ANDREW W. LIND
with the technical assistance of Robert Schmitt

MANUFACTURED IN THE UNITED STATES OF AMERICA

first edition, 1955

second edition, 1957, 1961

third edition, 1967

designed by Wendy Kim Chee

Somewhat over forty years have elapsed since the first publication by Romanzo Adams, as the senior author, of *The Peoples of Hawaii.* It was designed primarily to furnish the social scientists and administrators gathered in an international conference in Honolulu during the summer of 1925 with "information, mainly of a statistical nature, relating to the racial situation in Hawaii." Surviving members of that conference testify to the immediate usefulness of the small brochure of only forty-one pages, but it proved of even greater value during succeeding years to the residents of Hawaii and to scholars seeking a reliable and non-technical version of the process by which the many peoples of the Islands were becoming one people.

Nearly thirty years later another international conference of social scientists and administrators was held in Honolulu around the theme of "Race Relations in World Perspective" and this occasion presented even greater need for an informative account of Hawaii's experience with its diverse populations. The selection of Honolulu as the site for a conference with such global outreach was obviously made in part on the basis of the special interest of students of race relations in what has happened to the diverse peoples brought together in this mid-Pacific outpost over the preceding 150 years. Much of the data compiled in this study was presented in one way or another to the 1954 conferees from widely scattered portions of the world. The first edition of this volume sought, therefore, to parallel in some respects and to bring up to date the simple and informative account by Romanzo Adams and his collaborators in 1925, on the assumption that such an analysis would be no less revealing and significant thirty or forty years later. Notable developments which had occurred in the intervening years, especially those associated with the wars in the Pacific and in Korea, had so radically altered the Island situation and the relationships among the various ethnic groups as to justify a shift in the title of the study from *The Peoples of Hawaii* to *Hawaii's People.*

Publication in 1953 of the results of the 1950 decennial census made available a full century of more than usually reliable statistical data relating to the peoples who make up Hawaii's interesting racial melange. There are few regions anywhere in the world which afford such adequate census detail on the population changes throughout the period of racial contact and association. Only a small portion of these materials has been utilized in the present study, but it reflects the rich possibilities for further analysis.

The threatening nature of racial confrontations in many parts of the world, and not least in continental United States, gives added significance to a re-evaluation of the Hawaiian scene in the middle sixties. The intensification of racial conflicts in so many areas of the world following World War II tends to create an even greater aura of stability and calm about the Hawaiian experience. The relative absence in these islands of the violent expressions of racial animosities found elsewhere leads the unwary observer to the unwarranted assumption that Hawaii must possess some peculiar magic, whether in its people or the social climate, which might be exported to exorcise the evils of racism wherever they are found.

However inaccurate and misleading such characterizations may be, Hawaii's experimentation in race relations never fails to capture the attention of visitors to the Islands regardless of whether they approve or disapprove of what they see. Quite understandably, many of the more sophisticated observers from the critical areas of race relations in the world, including a number of participants in the 1954 conference, are frankly skeptical of what they contend must be the exaggerated claims of a Hawaiian racial utopia, and they admit seeking to find the flaws that clearly "must be there."

Data from the 1960 census provide the basis for further testing of the generalizations of the earlier edition of this study. Hawaii's achievement of the status as the fiftieth state of the Union in 1959 not only intensified the influences on the population and the economy from continental United States, but it also led to the introduction in the 1960 census of Mainland definitions of color and race which were at variance with Island tradition and the practice in earlier Island census counts. The most serious loss resulting from Statehood as it affects this particular study is the disappearance from most of the census reports of information relating to the more significant ethnic groups in Hawaii and the substitution of categories with respect to "color" which carry no significance whatsoever in the Island setting. Despite this serious limitation, there is in the 1960 census report much of value for charting the continuing trends in the interaction among the various groups called races in Hawaii.

Needless to say, it has not been the purpose of this study to support any preconception of Hawaiian race relations—either favorable or unfavorable. Rather an attempt has been made to bring together in readily understandable form some of the more important facts which limit, reflect, and measure the interaction among the peoples of Hawaii. Neither is there any assumption that generalizations derived from Hawaii's experience can be applied directly to the solution of problems of race relations in other areas of the world. Obviously, the way in which the peoples in Hawaii have come into being and have learned to live with one another cannot be dissociated from the entire social and economic situation of which they are a part, nor can the Hawaiian modes of living be applied without modification to continental United States, the Philippines, South Africa, or any other place.

On the other hand, many of the same principles of human interaction which govern race relations in Hawaii may be assumed to operate in other parts of the world, although their discovery and formulation require methods more involved than the simple statistical reporting chiefly used in this study. Hopefully the results of the more analytical and comparative study may be ready for publication within another year.

The author is especially indebted to Robert Schmitt, Hawaii State Statistician, for assistance in the preparation of several tables for the first edition and for valuable suggestions for the revision of the present edition. He is also grateful to Miss Katherine Toyota for the typing of the copy and to Mrs. Pamela Isayama for her editorial assistance.

ANDREW W. LIND

Honolulu, Hawaii
September, 1967

CONTENTS

HAWAII'S PEOPLE

INTRODUCTION

Adaptation to the shifting moods of nature was a constant require-ment for the survival of the earliest Polynesian settlers in Hawaii. So also experimentation and a readiness to change continue to be dominant themes in the economic and social life of these Islands following their discovery by Captain James Cook in 1778. For centuries the vast oceanic distances which separate Hawaii from its continental and larger island neighbors, coupled with the barren and volcanic nature of a large part of the limited land area, com-pelled the natives to utilize to the fullest the meager natural resources which were available to them.

These same limitations of mid-oceanic isolation and severely re-stricted land not only for the cultivation of crops but also as the very land base on which to live have not been eliminated, even with the benefits of ultra-modern agricultural and industrial technology and supersonic air travel. In the modern world, new complications owing to fluctuations in market demands for plantation crops, the recurring threats to world peace, and the unpredictable variations in fashions and recreational tastes among the masses demand even greater adaptability than did the threats of warfare, droughts, and the other hazards of nature in the pre-European era. Hawaii's economic and social history of the past century and a half can, therefore, be told largely in terms of the persistent search for more effective means of supporting human life and of capitalizing upon its limited material resources of land and sea within the context of a rapidly changing world community.

GEOGRAPHIC AND HISTORIC INFLUENCES

Hawaii's physical isolation, more than two thousand miles from its nearest continental neighbor, unquestionably contributed to the relatively late settlement of the Islands by their earliest Polynesian residents, estimated now to have occurred first in the tenth century A.D. That the Islands should have been discovered at all by the native peoples of the Pacific, considering their miniature vessels, the vast distances involved, and the lack of any prior knowledge of the existence of such lands, is still one of the unsolved mysteries of this largest of the world's oceans. It is all the more impressive considering how very late in the history of exploration by the Europeans, with their superior ships and technical knowledge of navigation, the modern discovery of Hawaii occurred.

The British search for a Northwest Passage from their colonies on the Pacific into the Atlantic was, of course, the occasion for the third voyage of Captain Cook into the unknown central Pacific, in the course of which the Hawaiian Islands were accidently encountered. So completely lost in the vast oceanic distances of the Pacific did Hawaii appear to be that the idea of claiming the Islands for his colonial-minded sovereign evidently did not occur to Cook, and he returned to Hawaii late in the fall of 1778 chiefly for the purpose of wintering in a milder climate and of replenishing his ships with the supplies of fresh fruit, vegetables, water, and fuel which were so readily accessible there. Even the knowledge of the larger land areas in Hawaii, discovered during Cook's return visit and made known to the Western world the following year, did not sufficiently tempt any of the land-hungry nations of Europe to seek the Islands for colonial purposes, and eight years elapsed before another foreign ship even ventured to visit them.

By virtue of the infinitesimal size of the land masses, which Cook named the Sandwich Islands in honor of his sponsor, and their effective isolation from the rest of the world, the Hawaiians were spared the fate of people in areas more conveniently situated for subjugation by one or another of the great imperial powers of the West. Had Captain Cook or any of the other European or American explorers and traders who visited Hawaii during the early years of Western contact conceived of Hawaii as offering much more than a desirable port of call for rest and replenishment on the long trek across the Pacific, the history of social relations in these islands would have taken quite a different course.

TRADE AND MISSIONS

The fact that Hawaii figured so prominently in the minds of Westerners as an outpost for trade rather than for colonial exploits is probably the one most critical factor in effecting the relatively peaceful and friendly relationships between the natives and foreigners in Hawaii, as compared with those in areas where colonialism and the use of Western military force have prevailed. The one serious breach in the peaceful relations between Captain Cook and the natives of Hawaii, ending in the death of the famous explorer, was the climax of a series of minor demonstrations of armed force and high-handedness by the crews of the *Discovery* and the *Resolution*, and fortunately even this tragic incident did not result in reprisals.

Subsequent visits from other British, American, Austrian, French, Russian, and Spanish explorers and traders further confirmed the tradition of equalitarian and peaceful relations. An occasional act of violence, such as the slaying in 1792 of four crew members of Captain George Vancouver's supply ship, the wanton slaughter of more than a hundred defenseless natives by an American trading captain in retaliation for the theft of one of his small boats, or the temporary seizure of the Islands by an over-zealous British admiral in 1843 might threaten but could not destroy the congenial relations between the Polynesians and the foreign visitors.

During most of the seventy years of contact prior to 1850, the values governing the relations between the *kanaka* (native) and the *haole* (foreigner) were those of the market place, characterized by the free and impersonal exchange of goods and services independent of color prejudice or cultural values. Each people had skills or goods which the other might desire, and neither group could afford to be disrespectful or obnoxious toward the other. The Westerner, if he wished to remain in the Islands, had to honor the customs and practices of the Hawaiians in their own country, and similarly, the natives would not abuse the foreigners whose goods and services they wished to enjoy. Moral and ethnic tolerance in Hawaii, as elsewhere, was at least in part a by-product of the market place.

A second set of circumstances conducive to effective working relations between the Westerners and the natives emanated from the missionary movement which began in 1820 with the arrival of the first seven married couples of New England Congregationalists. The Christian missionaries have been credited by some observers with establishing the tradition in Hawaii of equality and tolerance in human relations, and unquestionably their influence helped to stabilize this trend and to give it doctrinal support. It is not so commonly recognized that the missionaries came to Hawaii in the wake of and, to some degree, by the consent of the traders. Despite the bitter struggle between some of the traders and the missionaries for influence over the natives, these two groups of foreigners had very much in common and each drew support from the other. The missionaries, like the traders, were under obligation to the native rulers for their presence and well-being in the Islands, and neither their collective interests nor their professed doctrines would permit active discrimination against the natives.

Nurtured in a rigidly puritanical culture, the Protestant missionaries could hardly be expected to accept the indulgent and naturalistic practices of the natives, and missionary wives in particular sought to isolate their children from the contaminating influence of the Hawaiians. On the other hand, the religious faith they came to propagate in the Islands assumed the inherent value of all men in the sight of their God and a common claim to humane treatment. They could continue to be the relentless foes of "the iniquity and the scum of the ages," as they tended to conceive of native customs, and still insist upon the possible redemption of those who indulged in these practices.

Ambivalent though their sentiments might have been toward the natives and their culture, during the greater part of the nineteenth century the Protestant missionaries in Hawaii were strong supporters of political independence for the Islands and equalitarian relationships between Hawaiians and foreigners. Following the lead of William Richards, one of the early missionaries who in 1838 entered the employ of the king as adviser on matters relating to the State, they accepted important posts in the cabinet and loyally protected the interests of a native sovereign against the economic claims of Westerners and the political encroachments of foreign nations.

The Roman Catholic influence, dating from 1828, was less critical than the Protestant of native cultural idiosyncracies and also more receptive toward interracial marriage, particularly when it involved persons of the Catholic faith. The outlook of the Church of Jesus Christ of Latter Day Saints, introduced in Hawaii for the first time in 1848 and widely supported by the natives after its reception of them as members of one of the ten lost tribes of Israel, was possibly even more ascetic morally than that of the Protestants. The Mormons, like their Protestant and Catholic predecessors, also laid stress on the doctrine of human brotherhood regardless of race.

PLANTATIONS AND RACE RELATIONS

A third set of values introduced into Hawaii during the middle of the nineteenth century, in the form of plantation agriculture, threatened for a time to undermine the established pattern of human relationships. The plantation is, of course, first and foremost an economic institution designed to obtain maximum crop returns from idle or less effectively cultivated land on the frontier, but it also acquires a political and moral character through the necessary control over its labor force. In a region of "open resources" such as Hawaii, where the native population did not find it necessary or desirable to work on the plantations, the planters were compelled to seek their workers outside the Islands.

A whole series of previously untested ventures in induced immigration, sponsored by the Hawaiian government and the emerging plantation interests beginning at the middle of the last century and continuing over a period of nearly a hundred years, markedly altered the racial complexion of Hawaii's population and set the stage for an unprecedented experiment in race relations. Peoples of sharply contrasted ethnic and racial origins—Portuguese, Chinese, Puerto Ricans, Japanese, Micronesians, Melanesians, and Polynesians, Germans, Koreans, Russians, and Filipinos, among others—were imported in varying numbers to supply laborers for the expanding plantations of Hawaii, but with little thought for the complex processes of ethnic interaction which were thereby initiated.

Thus, in Hawaii, as in many other regions of the world, the demands of a plantation frontier for a substantial supply of disciplined labor was responsible for the repeopling of the region by foreigners. The native Polynesians, although tragically reduced by Western diseases from about 300,000 at the time of the Islands' discovery to 84,000 in 1850, obviously could have provided sufficient workers for the developing plantation enterprises, had they been so disposed. There was, however, little reason for the Hawaiians to offer themselves as plantation laborers under the onerous and confining conditions which prevailed—long hours of hard labor under driving rain and hot tropical sun—when all their personal needs and desires could be quite adequately and much more pleasantly satisfied at home. The foreigners who sought to gain a fortune from the unused agricultural lands of Hawaii had no choice but to seek their workers from regions outside the Islands, thus laying the foundations for the racial melange which now constitutes Hawaii's population.

Toward the beginning of the plantation era, at the time of the

1850 census, Hawaii's total population was reported as 84,165, of whom 82,035 were supposedly pure Hawaiians. The other 2,130 persons were largely adventurers from all parts of the globe— American and French missionaries, traders and seamen from such widely separated regions as Africa, China, Brazil, the United States, Denmark, the Philippines, and Turkey—and somewhat over 500 persons of mixed Hawaiian ancestry. The European and American planters, despairing of securing from among the natives the type of "willing and industrious" workers they required, turned first to China, which might easily have served as an inexhaustible reservoir for their future demands. The need for effective labor control, however, dictated a policy of drawing the workers from a number of different sources, and after a few years of experimentation with a predominantly Chinese labor force, the Hawaiian planters were careful to avoid dependence upon workers of any one ethnic group.

Over a time span of nearly a century from the middle of the nineteenth century, the planters of Hawaii, with some encouragement from the government, recruited more than 400,000 persons from the four corners of the earth as plantation workers or their dependents. In their initial role as the unskilled laborers in the fields, the immigrants were regarded much like draft animals, and their recognition as normal human beings ordinarily occurred only after months or years of contact. Involved considerations, including the costs of recruiting and transporting the workers, their labor efficiency and tractability, and matters of political expendiency were determining factors in the particular selection of the ethnic types, distributed roughly in the following numbers: 180,000 from Japan proper and Okinawa; 125,000 from the Tagalog, Visayan, and Ilocos provinces of the Philippines; 46,000 South Chinese; 17,500 Portuguese from the Azores and the Madeira Islands; 8,000 Koreans; 6,000 Puerto Ricans; 8,000 Spaniards; 1,300 Germans and Galicians; 2,500 Islanders from widely separated areas in the Pacific; 2,000 Russians; and numerous other groups in smaller numbers.

The fact that Hawaii could attract immigrants in such numbers and from such varied areas was perhaps more a consequence of the adverse economic conditions in the countries of origin than of the superior financial inducements or working conditions which Hawaii's plantations had to offer. Despite the disillusionment of long hours of monotonous and physically exhausting labor at meager wages, large numbers of these labor recruits continued to find greater economic opportunities and a more pleasant life in Hawaii than in their homelands, and with their Island-born children they still constitute well over half of Hawaii's population.

It was, in brief, through the plantations that the first clearly defined pattern of stratification by race was introduced into Hawaii. During most of the sixty-year period prior to World War II, when sugar and pineapple production dominated Hawaii's economic life, a fairly distinct barrier of social distances separated the proprietary whites from the large mass of nonwhite laborers on the plantation, and a further isolation of the ethnic groups at the lower levels of the plantation occupational pyramid also emerged.

That the social hierarchy within the plantation communities of Hawaii never attained the rigidity of a caste structure, as on similar frontiers elsewhere in the world, is largely a consequence of the strong competition of Hawaii's well established trading and commercial centers, to which a dissatisfied plantation worker could escape. Moreover as the Hawaiian economy has shifted from one in which labor was scarce to one in which it is relatively plentiful, the necessity of maintaining a rigid system of control through ethnic barriers has also tended to decline. Under the modern conditions of a highly mechanized economy which requires far less unskilled labor, the earlier labor controls can be relaxed and workers, regardless of ethnic origin, may be permitted to advance into occupational positions on the basis of individual merit.

POLITICAL AND MILITARY FORCES

Still another set of influences affecting the class and ethnic structure of the Islands from the middle of the nineteenth century onward has been introduced by American political and military forces. American commercial interests in the Islands, desirous of safeguarding their own investments and of securing special legal advantages by incorporation within the American commonwealth, had openly agitated for annexation as early as 1850. Like other foreign nationals in Hawaii, American residents had even earlier sought the intervention of foreign gunboats to enforce their claims against Hawaiian chiefs and royalty. Although Americans and other foreigners, operating openly or behind the scenes, had significantly influenced the policies of the Hawaiian Kingdom during most of the century, it was not until 1893 that the vestiges of native control were finally abandoned.

The transfer of sovereignty to the United States in 1898 was naturally deplored by many Hawaiians and Part-Hawaiians as a public confession that the native people could not manage their own

bill introduced in December 1898 in the U. S. Congress
charter and constitution for Hawaii restricted citizenship
te persons, including Portuguese and persons of African
descent, and all persons descended from the Hawaiian race on
either the paternal or maternal side, who were citizens of the
Republic of Hawaii immediately prior to the transfer of sovereignty
thereof to the United States." As it was finally signed into law
by President McKinley in April 1900, the Organic Act contained
the same phraseology but omitted any reference to race, nationality,
or descent, and it provided for the application of the American
constitutional guarantees of equality before the law regardless of
racial ancestry. On the other hand, federal legislation supported by
Mainland racial attitudes excluded from citizenship and participation
in the political life of the Territory large portions of the residents of
Oriental ancestry, and it was not until after World War II that a
major shift in the nation's conception of itself brought the laws
to partially correct this form of racial discrimination. National sentiments adverse to the equalitarian racial practices in the Islands
likewise contributed to the retention of Hawaii in a subordinate
political status for nearly sixty years, when objective criteria would
have justified the granting of Statehood a decade or two earlier.

The direct impact of the armed forces upon the social structure
in Hawaii was not particularly noticeable until after 1920, at which
time there were less than 4,000 military personnel in the Islands.
The threat of war and the mounting military preparations, culminat-
ing in the four years of actual warfare in which Hawaii was the
focal point of American military strategy in the Pacific, introduced
almost overnight a new defense population, surpassing in numbers
the permanent residents of the Islands.

Faced with an Island population which in physical appearance
and in many of its practices was largely unfamiliar, the newly
arrived servicemen and defense workers during World War II were
prone to regard most of the residents with suspicion, applying to
any non-Caucasian such invidious terms as "gook," "nigger," "slant-
eyes," or "yellow-belly." Quite understandably the non-Caucasian
Islanders responded in like fashion with "white-trash" or "damn
haole." Moreover, in their search for feminine companionship, the
enlisted men tended to cross ethnic lines and thus to invade the local
preserves, inevitably drawing forth the resentment, and sometimes
violence, of Island males whose attentions had been rejected by their
former girl friends. Even under the less competitive conditions since

the war, when the numbers of military personnel have been greatly reduced and their wives and children have been permitted to come to Hawaii, such animosities have persisted and to some degree threatened the relative calm of the Islands.

At the time of the 1960 census nearly 8.3 per cent of Hawaii's total population were in the military services, and together with their dependents, they constituted 17.7 per cent of the total. With military expenditures in Hawaii in recent years surpassing the income from all agricultural sources and constituting the largest single source of income, it might be expected that military conceptions of rank, as applied also to the racial complexity of Hawaii's population, would be more widely observed in the larger Island community. Insofar as the military and civilian populations have been able to intermingle, however, the preponderant influence has been toward the preservation of the Island pattern of race relations, and in the areas of normal association outside the military reservations, it has been the newcomers who have found it desirable "when in Hawaii to do as the Hawaiians do."

TOURISM

During the first third of this century, the plantation economy, with its significant impact on both the ethnic complexion and the social structure of the Islands, had reached and passed its peak. There was no additional unused land into which the plantations could expand, federal quotas limited the tonnage of sugar which could be marketed in the U. S., and the competition of foreign producers cut seriously into the profitable market for Island pineapples. In the meantime another source of income and a potentially disturbing force in Hawaii's pattern of race relations appeared in the form of tourism.

The increasing speed and declining costs of air travel following World War II, together with the mounting incomes in much of the Western world, have precipitated an even larger influx of temporary visitors, chiefly from the U. S. Mainland. This flood of tourists, rising steadily until their number in the mid-sixties surpassed that of the resident civilian population, has brought into being an economy designed to entertain, divert, and indulge the creature comforts of "outsiders." How successfully the Islanders schooled in the values of a productive economy will be able to adapt to the requirements of a tourist economy is not yet fully apparent, but there can be little doubt that for the foreseeable future tourism will continue to expand and that an increasing proportion of Hawaii's people will be oriented to its development.

From only 15,000 visitors in 1946, the annual flow of tourists had swelled to 109,800 persons in 1955 and to nearly 600,000 ten years later, and the tourist industry now exceeds either sugar or pineapples as a source of Hawaii's gross income. The sheer number of visitors involved, almost certain to reach one million per year by 1970, and the mounting weight of their financial expenditures are bound to have profound, but as yet somewhat unpredictable, consequences upon the life of the Islands. Like the military, the tourist tends to arrive in Hawaii with the racial attitudes and prejudices of his home community, but to a greater degree than the military, the tourist is seeking new experiences and sometimes an escape from the confining values of family and friends. In his search of adventure and stimulation, therefore, the tourist is also amenable to change, and he may discard with surprising ease his earlier prejudices as being unsuitable in the new environment. Among so large a number of visitors, the great diversity in types on the basis of age, sex, and social class alone suggest caution, however, in predicting what their total impact will be.

Thus within the relatively brief period since World War II, Hawaii's economy and the population supported by it have experienced a series of far-reaching transformations, in some respects as revolutionary as that initiated in 1778 when Captain Cook penetrated for the first time the stone-age existence of the Islands. Within less than a generation, the plantation as the major source of Hawaii's income had been displaced from its dominant position. For a short time during the thirties, it seemed possible that the plantations might successfully compete with the expanding military forces for first place, and the characterization of Hawaii as a "Sugar-Coated Fortress" seemed most appropriate. After the Pearl Harbor attack the old order was clearly forced into a secondary role, and a new era of experimentation in human relations was initiated.

SHIFTING HUMAN FRONTIERS

Contrary to the usual impression held by visitors to Hawaii and many residents, the Island pattern of social organization is far from simple. The influence of each of the agencies just enumerated— the center of trade, the Christian mission, the plantation, the military establishment, or the tourist center—is never unitary or exclusive. Each affects the others and is in turn influenced by them. In addition to the factors already outlined, a number of important variables serve to increase the complexity of the Island scene.

The peculiar selection of population types which has occurred in Hawaii provides the first and perhaps most important modifying influence upon the local social scene. Beginning with the specialized branch of Polynesians native to the Islands at the time of discovery by the West, Hawaii has attracted a unique combination of Occidental and Oriental peoples which, in terms of the proportions and circumstances involved, is duplicated nowhere in the world. The significance of this selection becomes more apparent when one considers the probable effect on Hawaiian history if British or Russian traders had become dominant in the Islands instead of Yankee merchants, or if African or European labor markets had been more extensively tapped than those of Asia. Equally striking has been the effect upon Hawaii's economic and social life of the introduction of a predominantly male population from China, Korea, and the Philippines in contrast to the more normal sex proportions among the immigrants from Japan and Portugal. Such considerations will be elaborated in the second chapter of this study.

The effects of mid-oceanic isolation on Hawaii's political destiny have already been briefly outlined. The further consequences of insularity within the Islands will be more thoroughly explored in Chapter 3. It is fairly obvious, however, that the more fertile and agriculturally productive sections of the major islands have been largely preempted by sugar and pineapple plantations with their large concentrations of immigrant labor groups, while the arid and less suitable agricultural lands have provided a haven for a disproportionate number of the remaining native Hawaiians. In addition the rural areas, depending somewhat on the nature of the soil, elevation, rainfall, and the accessibility to markets, have developed other types of economies, such as ranching or small scale agriculture, with their specialized selections of ethnic groups and relationships between them.

The more suitable oceanic harbors on the various islands, including Honolulu, Hilo, Wailuku, and Lihue, as well as other crossroads of transportation, are the natural areas of concentration for the rising middle class from various ethnic backgrounds. They provide the atmosphere for freer experimentation in human relations than is possible elsewhere in the Islands. The city has always been a haven for those who could not adjust readily to the more rigid patterns of economic and racial stratification in the rural areas.

Here also occurs the curious development of voluntary racial ghettoes, or "camps" as they are more commonly called in Hawaii, where the immigrant can hear his native tongue, see familiar faces, and enjoy contact with those who understand him. But it is also in the city that avenues of contact across ethnic lines are most open and free and that the breakdown of ethnic controls proceeds most rapidly.

A remote island, and especially an extended group of small islands, always places severe limits on the economic and occupational prospects for its residents. On the other hand, the Hawaiian Islands have been a land of far greater opportunity than the homelands from which the majority of its immigrants came. The effect of opening Hawaii to the world channels of trade has been to increase greatly the economic wealth of the Islands, and, as a consequence, a greatly expanded population has found ample means of livelihood. Furthermore, the economic opportunities have not been confined to the bottom rungs of the economic ladder for the large number of workers imported by the plantations. Although many of the labor immigrants have preferred to return to their native countries to spend their later years, others have found in Hawaii the means of a higher plane of living and of vocational and social satisfactions denied them in their native lands. Some of the quantitative data to support this story will be set forth in greater detail in Chapter 4.

Another area of social adjustment in which all of Hawaii's people have become involved to a greater or lesser degree is commonly referred to by sociologists as assimilation. As a consequence of living together within a common economic region and engaging in the interaction which that fact entails, people of diverse cultural and racial antecedents inevitably come to acquire certain common practices and outlooks on life. The barriers created by aversion toward the offensively different in other cultures and by strong loyalties to the traditional values of the ancestral homeland gradually lose their influence even on the immigrants, and more so on their children. The process of building a new set of values appropriate to the Island scene is naturally one which requires above all else time—generations—to accomplish. But there are other essentials too for assimilation, including attitudes of adaptability and acceptance and a social situation conducive to free interchange among the groups involved, and in these respects there are bound to be important differentials in the speed and effectiveness of the process. Some of the more obvious evidences of this process and of the conditions under which it takes place will be outlined in Chapter 5.

2

WHO ARE THEY?

Change has been a dominant characteristic of almost every aspect of Island life throughout the period since the middle of the last century, but it is especially apparent in the ethnic character and complexion of the people. Hawaii, whose declining population in 1850 was still predominantly Polynesian in composition, rapidly acquired sizeable additions of people from various parts of Asia, the South and Western Pacific, the Atlantic Ocean area, the Caribbean, as well as the continental United States. As recently as 1935, Romanzo Adams [1] could accurately write about Hawaii as a land of many peoples, and the conception still remains that a colorful variation in racial types and in cultural survivals continues to be Hawaii's most distinctive social attribute and one of its major charms for visitors. On the other hand, a fusion of racial types and a blending of cultures within what was popularly, although inappropriately, called "the Hawaiian melting pot" had become increasingly apparent and represented the trend in which Adams was chiefly interested. These are the major trends to be observed in the present chapter.

THE NATIVE HAWAIIANS

The available evidence indicates that the inhabitants of these islands at the time of their discovery by Westerners were a healthy, viable folk whose ancestors might have first arrived from their south Pacific home islands as much as a thousand years earlier. The natural resources of both land and sea were probably being cultivated to the maximum within the limitations of a stone-age tech-

[1]Romanzo Adams, *The Peoples of Hawaii* (Honolulu: The Institute of Pacific Relations, 1933), p. 5.

nology. Prior to the coming of the white man, Hawaii was clearly a region of closed resource, where cultivable land was at a premium and population was limited only by the available supply of food.

Like most of the Pacific islands of isolated folk peoples, Hawaii suffered a tragic decline in its native population following contact with the West. Assuming, according to the best available knowledge, that Hawaii's indigenous population could not have been much in excess of 300,000 at the time of Captain Cook's visit in 1778, a disastrous loss in human resources occurred within seventy-five years. The first complete official census of the Islands in 1853 reported a total of 71,019 native Hawaiians, or less than a quarter of the pre-European figure. Small wonder that the missionaries were fearful lest the native population become extinct before the close of the century and that they were encouraged to labor even harder in the Lord's vineyard so as to "seize as many as possible of the burning brands before they were consumed in the eternal fires." Missionary reports to their American sponsors assumed at times a fatalistic outlook toward a people doomed of God—that "the waning of the people admonishes us to do all in our power to prepare them for a speedy removal from earthly scenes."

The factors responsible for the abnormally high death rates and the correspondingly low birth rates which must have prevailed during the first half of the nineteenth century in Hawaii have been discussed at considerable length elsewhere [2] and need not be elaborated further here. Actually the data from which to compute vital rates for this period are not available, but it was obvious to the most casual observer that the Hawaiians at that time were "a dying people"—the victims of Western diseases to which they had not yet developed an immunity. On the basis of a careful reworking of missionary counts conducted in 1823 and in 1836, Romanzo Adams indicates that due to an excess of deaths over births the number of native Hawaiians may have declined a staggering 20 per cent in approximately thirteen years. During the four years between the two missionary enumerations of 1832 and 1836, there was an even more alarming decline from 124,449 to 107,954, or 13.2 per cent which, if it had continued unabated, would have brought about the extinction of the Hawaiian within a generation. An average annual decline of 2 per cent continued during the next seventeen

[2] Andrew W. Lind, *An Island Community* (Chicago: The University of Chicago Press, 1938), pp. 93-99; Bernhard L. Hormann, "Rigidity and Fluidity in Race Relations," in A. W. Lind, ed., *Race Relations in World Perspective* (Honolulu: University of Hawaii Press, 1955), pp. 25-48.

years, bringing the native population down to a figure of 71,019 by 1853.[3]

The decrease in the number of native Hawaiians continued for another fifty years, although at a somewhat reduced rate. Between 1853 and 1896 the total Hawaiian population, including those of mixed ancestry, dropped still further to 39,504, or at an annual average of slightly more than 1 per cent. During part of this period, particularly from 1860 to 1872, the rate of decline continued at about 2 per cent annually, and it was not until after 1890 that the native Hawaiian population became somewhat stabilized. Actually the lowest level in this downward trend was reached shortly after 1900, although a significant reversal was not apparent until the second decade of the present century.

What happened to the native population during the first half of the twentieth century is just as dramatic as the awful decimation which occurred during the whole of the previous century. Not only was the population decline effectively halted, but a neo-Hawaiian group, composed of Hawaiians and Part-Hawaiians, began to establish itself as the most rapidly growing people within the Islands. It is true that this rejuvenated racial stock contains a slowly diminishing remnant of the pure Hawaiians, destined in time to disappear entirely, but the Polynesian stamp and influence is very definitely marked upon those *keiki o ka aina*—children of the land—who are known as Hawaiians. Beginning with the census of 1920, there is evidence of a distinct increase in the population of Hawaiian ancestry, although this obviously would not be true except for the Island practice of classifying all persons with any Hawaiian ancestry as members of that group. A slight increase of 3,203, or 8.3 per cent, between 1910 and 1920 was followed by a 21.8 per cent rise in population during the following decade and a growth of slightly more than 25 per cent during both the thirties and forties.

The striking reversal in the population trend among the native Polynesian peoples in Hawaii is attributable to several major factors which we can only mention here. The establishment of a program of Western preventive medicine, symbolized by the founding of a board of health in 1851, had increasing effect in reducing the deaths from the epidemic diseases which took such a harrowing toll during the first half of the century. At the same time the native Hawaiians were slowly learning the value of Western medicine and

[3]Romanzo Adams, *Interracial Marriage in Hawaii* (New York: The Macmillan Company, 1937), p. 8.

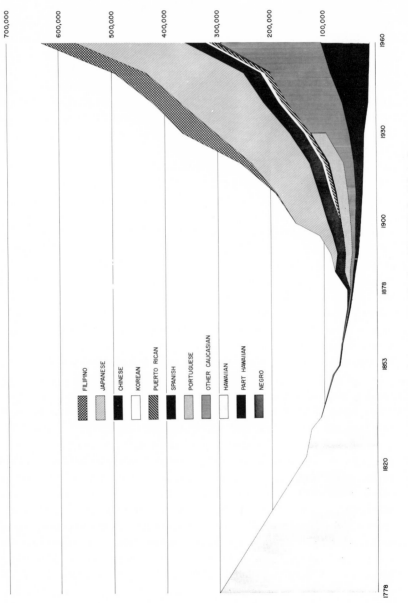

Figure 1. Population of the Hawaiian Islands, 1778–1960, by Ethnic Groups

were changing their mode of life accordingly. Some immunity to the diseases introduced from the West was also being built up among the natives during the same period.

A final factor in the deliverance of the Hawaiian race was the growing intermarriage of the natives with the numerous ethnic groups which were attracted to the Islands. As early as 1853 nearly a thousand persons, or slightly more than 1 per cent of the total population, were listed in the census as "Hapahaole" or "Part native." By the close of the century, the number of Hawaiians of mixed ancestry recorded by the census had increased to nearly ten thousand and they constituted more than a quarter of all the Hawaiians in the Islands. Even before 1930, the Part-Hawaiians had exceeded the "pure" Hawaiians in numbers, and since that time, among all those who claim to be Hawaiians, the ratio of Part-Hawaiians has increased so much that according to the 1960 census they represented 89 per cent of the total. The combined Hawaiian and Part-Hawaiian population increased at the strikingly high average rate of 3.5 per cent annually during the twenty-year period from 1930 to 1950. Although this dropped to 1.9 per cent during the following decade, owing to extensive out-migrations, the rate of natural increase by the excess of births over deaths continued at a high of 4.2 per cent annually, which far exceeded that of any other ethnic group. Far from being a "dying race," as they seemed to be during most of the nineteenth century, the Hawaiians are now the Islands' most rapidly expanding ethnic group.

IMMIGRANT PEOPLES—THE CHANGING DEFINITIONS

Hawaii's reputation as a laboratory in human relations dates chiefly from the second half of the nineteenth century when large-scale immigration to meet the plantation labor demands began. In 1853, the foreign population of 2,119 persons was largely concentrated in the half-dozen trading centers scattered over the various islands, and was as varied in racial composition as the communities around the world at which the visiting trading and whaling vessels might previously have stopped. Some thirty-three different countries or regions, including the United States, Great Britain, Ireland, Holland, Germany, Turkey, Brazil, Africa, China, Australasia, and the Philippines, were separately listed in the census as contributing to the cosmopolitan population of the Islands.

It is significant that the foreigners in Hawaii a century ago were classified according to the cultural groups to which they belonged.

They were apparently known as Americans, British, French, Chinese, and Hawaiians or natives, and were not classified in racial terms such as white, yellow, and brown. This practice has continued to a degree until the present day and symbolizes the dominant attitude in Hawaii of indifference to race. Indeed, it was not until after Annexation that Mainland conceptions of race were partially introduced in the census practices of Hawaii.

Differences in language, food habits, dress, and moral values could hardly be disregarded in the case of foreigners drawn from such widely varied portions of the earth. The early immigrants from China, with their prominent queues and black pantaloons, their strange language, and peculiar modes of living, were bound to stand out strikingly from the natives and the Europeans, and some type of differentiation was inevitable as long as the alien practices persisted. So each of the immigrant groups—Norwegians, Germans, Portuguese, Japanese, Koreans, or Puerto Ricans—were known by their own cultural or national label as long as they continued to observe habits of eating, dressing, speaking, housing themselves, or worshipping which definitely marked them off from the rest of the population.

A considerable number of the cultural or national groups from northwestern Europe and from America already possessed a common body of customs and were sufficiently alike in appearance to be regarded as a single group. This unity of Europeans and Americans who settled in Hawaii was further emphasized by the fact that many of them were skilled artisans, professionals, or tradesmen and hence enjoyed positions of prestige and affluence within the emerging economy of the Islands.

The Hawaiian term "haole" (stranger) was applied by the natives to all the visitors to the Islands, and according to Romanzo Adams,[4] it did not refer to color at all during the early period of contact with the West. Since most of the early visitors were white-complexioned persons who exercised considerable power in the frontier community, the term "haole" increasingly came to denote exclusively influential and wealthy persons of North European and American ancestry. West European immigrants such as most of the Portuguese and Spanish and many of the Norwegians and Germans, who were brought to Hawaii as ordinary plantation workers, were not classified as Haoles until they had emerged from the category of unskilled labor into positions of middle- or upper-class status.

4*Ibid.*, p. 115.

The class unity implied in the term "haole" was not, however, during most of the nineteenth century sufficient to counteract the social and cultural differences between such groups as the British, French, and Americans, and it was not until after Annexation that they were combined in the census classifications as a single group, with something of a racial connotation.

Race, in the traditional Western sense of a large grouping of human beings distinguished from others by identifiable and biologically inherited physical traits, scarcely functioned among the great mass of Hawaii's people during most of the nineteenth century. National origin or nationality was the classificatory device used instead of race in most of the eight censuses conducted during the second half of the century. A footnote in the 1853 census report, reflecting the prevailing lack of race consciousness, states that nineteen Negroes were included among the foreigners resident in Honolulu, but no attempt was made to differentiate them from the rest of the population. Similarly, at a later date when the number of Hawaii-born children of foreigners became large enough to necessitate a separate census category, no distinction was made among them on the basis of race or ancestry. Children of Chinese, Portuguese, Japanese, Micronesian, or English parentage were all included within a common classification. The nearest approximation to a conventional designation of race in biological terms appeared in the censuses from 1866 to 1890 in the use of the term "half-caste" for persons of mixed Hawaiian ancestry.

The collapse of the native monarchy and a mounting American influence during the period of the Republic, climaxed in 1898 with annexation of Hawaii to the United States, brought an increased awareness of the racial practices of the American mainland and some tendency to emulate them. Thus, in the first population census taken after Annexation, Mainland racial definitions were applied to Hawaii's people, resulting in the combining of Haoles and Portuguese, as well as several thousand light-complexioned Part-Hawaiians, under the imported term of Caucasians. This practice was modified in 1910 so as to take account of local distinctions between Haoles and the plantation-imported Portuguese and Spanish. The biologically tinged racial term of Caucasian was retained, however, as a permanent acquisition from the Mainland and was subsequently taken over by the Territorial Bureau of Vital Statistics in its intercensal estimates of population. Persons of European or American ancestry enjoying Haole status were classified separately under the anomalous designation of "Other Caucasians." Another curious consequence of the introduction of American racial terminology was the inclusion of the immigrants from Puerto Rico as a separate category under Caucasians, although persons from continental United States with any Negro admixture were placed in a category new for Hawaii—that of "Negro." It is also likely that Mainland conceptions of race were chiefly responsible for the new distinction between two types of Part-Hawaiians, subsequently known as Caucasian-Hawaiians and Asiatic-Hawaiians.

During the first half of the present century, Hawaii vacillated somewhat in the terminology applied to its people, sometimes accepting the imported implication of biologically inherited differences between its immigrant peoples but more commonly adhering to the Island assumption that these observed differences are culturally acquired and may also disappear. The terms usually applied, such as Chinese, Japanese, Korean, Filipino, Portuguese, Spanish, Samoan, and Puerto Rican, refer to the country of origin and, like the dress of the immigrant, may be abandoned for a Hawaiian or an American one. Thus, in conformity with Island expectations and practice,[5] the earlier division among Portuguese, Spanish, and "Other Caucasians" was officially abandoned in 1940, and at the same time, the Asiatic-Hawaiians and the Caucasian-Hawaiians were combined in a single group of Part-Hawaiians.

Official agencies, such as the Police Department and the State Departments of Social Services, Health, and of Education, have followed different variants of the two principles mentioned above. The Police Department, for example, still differentiates between Caucasian- and Asiatic-Hawaiians, while also taking account of Portuguese and Spanish, as well as the other more commonly recognized immigrant groups—Chinese, Filipinos, Japanese, Koreans, and Puerto Ricans. For many years, the Department of Public Instruction kept its records of the school children of the Territory in terms of "racial ancestry," specifying at various times separate categories for "Anglo-Saxons," and "Americans" in place of "Haoles" or "Other Caucasians." A growing sentiment that racial designations are inconsistent with the democratic professions of the American public school system was responsible in 1945 for the complete abandonment of the system of reporting school enrollment by race, although effec-

---

[5]This reflects the situation in the urban centers, where attitudes favorable to the free participation of all the ethnic groups in the life of the community have been most highly developed. In many of the plantation communities, Portuguese are still regarded as a separate ethnic group.

tive personnel work has apparently necessitated keeping a record of the racial ancestry of each child. Much the same policy has been followed in recent years by the Department of Social Services with regard to its clients.

Certain other agencies, including some of the public institutions for correction and treatment, have found it advantageous to differentiate among the numerous types of mixed bloods which have come into being, especially during the twentieth century. The ludicrous extremes to which an excessive interest in race, biologically defined, can force one in Hawaii is reflected in the report of one agency which a few years ago listed 169 different racial groups in its constituency, including such complex combinations as Portuguese-Caucasian-Negro-Puerto Rican, Chinese-Hawaiian-Japanese-Norwegian, Filipino-Puerto Rican-Spanish, and Filipino-Hawaiian-Japanese-Puerto Rican-Portuguese. A recently completed study of the "Genetics of Interracial Crosses in Hawaii" indicates that, if account is taken of eight major racial groups and twenty-two biracial or multiracial combinations recognized in that research alone, making thirty groups for each parent, the potential number of resulting mating types would be nine hundred, of which 524 different types were actually discovered in the analysis of all births in the Islands between 1948 and 1958.

It was to forestall such statistical anomalies that the United States Census Bureau and the Territorial Bureau of Vital Statistics in the 1930's adopted certain principles regarding the classification of persons of mixed ancestry. Thus, a person of any Hawaiian ancestry no matter how slight the admixture of native blood, if it is recognized and known, is designated as Part-Hawaiian.[6] A second principle specifies that any person of both Caucasian and non-Caucasian ancestry (other than Hawaiian) shall be classified in the group of his non-Caucasian parent, if it is recognized in Hawaii. Thus, the child of a Caucasian father and a Japanese mother is designated as Japanese.[7] On the basis of a third principle, the child of two racially different non-Caucasian and non-Hawaiian parents is classified according to the race of the father. These rules, although useful in sorting people into convenient statistical groups, are obviously quite

[6]Since 1950, Part-Hawaiians have been included with pure Hawaiians in most of the census tables.

[7]As Bernhard Hormann points out, this assumes the "racial purity" of the Caucasians, even though they "may be compounded of various European mixtures, such as Portuguese, Russian, English, German." " 'Racial' Statistics in Hawaii," *Social Process in Hawaii*, XII (1948), 29.

arbitrary, and under conditions of extensive crossing of racial lines, they can result in great confusion.

During the early period of immigrant settlement in Hawaii, including the last half of the nineteenth century and the first three decades of the present century, there was relatively little crossing of the conventional race lines, except with the Hawaiians and Part-Hawaiians. As a consequence, the census figures provided an accurate reflection of the numerical size and character of each of the immigrant racial groups. The Hawaiians and Part-Hawaiians still play the most prominent part in the amalgamative process in the Islands, but a growing tendency to disregard racial consideration in marriage during the period since World War II naturally raised doubts as to the adequacy of the census returns on race. A request was therefore submitted to the Census Bureau to introduce a new question in the 1950 enumeration, designed to discover the extent of racial crossing in the Islands. The rationale behind this proposal was stated as follows:

A change in census practice so as to take account of the mounting population of mixed ancestry—both those with some Hawaiian blood and those with no known Hawaiian blood—would serve to increase the accuracy of our population reporting and it would moreover be more nearly in conformity with local sentiment regarding race relations. Public sentiment has, in general, been sympathetic to intermarriage and the conception of Hawaii as "a melting pot of the races" finds public support. It is a source of local pride that Hawaii's many immigrant stocks are gradually losing their separate identity and are becoming "one people" and any system of reporting which would more accurately reflect this process of Americanization is likely to be favorably received in Hawaii.

Barring unforeseen developments, within another generation Hawaii's population will be predominantly of mixed racial ancestry and the time has already come when the census enumeration should provide an accurate measure of this trend. The year 1950 provides a natural point of transition between the first half of the century when attention was still focused primarily upon the immigrant stocks and the second half of the century when the emphasis will be chiefly upon the fusion of these stocks into a common American whole. The proposals for the 1950 census of population would yield accurate information as to the passing of the immigrant stocks and the growth of a new population which is neither Asiatic nor European but peculiarly Hawaiian and American.[8]

The added question on racial mixture yielded less impressive results than had been anticipated. The predominance of mixed bloods among the Hawaiians was clearly substantiated, and there is some reason to

[8]*Final Report of Census Subcommittee on Population Characteristics and Occupation* (Honolulu: Chamber of Commerce of Honolulu, 1949), pp. 3-4.

believe, as Romanzo Adams has pointed out, that "Part-Hawaiians, especially the darker complexioned ones, frequently are ignorant of their possession of non-Hawaiian blood or they think that their little non-Hawaiian blood is of no practical importance, and so they claim to be full blooded Hawaiians." [9] Adams estimated that in 1930 the number of pure Hawaiians was 12,856, which would make the figure of 12,206 in 1950 seem unduly high.

1. RACE MIXTURE

	TOTAL	UNMIXED	MIXED	
			Number	Per Cent
Hawaiian	86,091	12,206	73,885	85.8
Caucasian	114,793	114,793		
Chinese	32,376	29,501	2,875	8.9
Filipino	61,071	53,391	7,680	12.6
Japanese	184,611	180,521	4,090	2.2
Other Races	20,852	15,160	5,692	27.3
TOTAL	499,794	405,572	94,222	18.9

It is reasonable to assume that similar errors in classification, but to a lesser degree, may appear in the data of other groups reported in Table 1, but the ratios of mixed ancestry conform roughly with what one would expect on the basis of records of interracial marriage and births. Unfortunately comparable data are not available for 1960, but if the 1950 figures are even moderately accurate, they leave little doubt as to the legitimate place for racial statistics in the case of the larger groups for some years to come.

The granting of statehood in 1959 resulted in the arbitrary application to Hawaii in the census of 1960 of the same rules of racial classification that were used in continental United States. Thus the alien conception of race as identified with color was introduced into all of the 1960 census reports on Hawaii. The statement in the published volumes of the 1960 United States Census of Population under the heading of "Race and Color" implies that color is simply the more inclusive term covering one or more races and that of the two primary classifications most widely used in the census, white and nonwhite, the latter combines such "races" as Negro, American Indian, Japanese, Chinese, Filipino, Korean, Asian Indian, Eskimo, and Hawaiian.[10]

[9]Adams, *Interracial Marriage in Hawaii*, p. 14.
[10]Bureau of the Census, *Census of Population: 1960*, Vol. I, Part 13 (Washington: Government Printing Office, 1963), p. xx.

As a consequence, the published reports of the 1960 census of Hawaii contain table after table—some eighty-two of them—of involved data differentiating solely between white and nonwhite populations, with the latter category, of course, being virtually meaningless and unusable. On the other hand, the limited number of tables providing data by racial groups takes account only of the categories most meaningful in continental United States—white, Negro, and "other races"—with a further breakdown of the latter into the groupings which are meaningful in Hawaii confined to only three tables out of a total of 146 published. It is possible to extract from a separate volume dealing with the entire United States, entitled *Nonwhite Population by Race*, a severely restricted body of data relating to only three of our major ethnic groups in Hawaii— the Chinese, Japanese, and Filipinos. The areas of information relating to these three groups, however, are much more limited than in earlier census returns, and this fact explains the absence of 1960 data in many of the tables and the text in later portions of this book.

Despite the pressures from outside the Islands to characterize and classify Hawaii's people in racial groupings biologically conceived as sharing common, identifiable, and genetically transmitted physical traits, the ethnic groups of which people actually take account have social and cultural bases in addition to those of a physiological nature. The so-called races of Hawaii are in reality groupings of people—frequently immigrants and their children—sharing common cultural and physical traits by which they can be identified. Thus the racial distinctions in Hawaii have appeared when there has been an awareness that the immigrant peoples and the natives are significantly different in physical appearance, economic position and class, or any set of social practices; the distinctions have disappeared when people subsequently lost that awareness.

IMMIGRANT PEOPLES—THE CHANGING FACTS

It is against such a background of "unorthodox" and changing conceptions of race that the various immigrant groups have been introduced into Hawaii. The Chinese, the first of the numerous ethnic types to be brought in for plantation purposes, constituted the dominant source of labor supply during the last half of the nineteenth century. The numbers involved were relatively small until the late seventies, when the rapid influx of Chinese began to alarm seriously even some of the planters, who were fearful lest a labor monopoly be created to threaten the entire plantation system. The unexpected arrival early in 1883 of a steamship from Hong Kong loaded with Chinese for Hawaii, followed immediately by three more shiploads and reports of others on the way, stirred even the *Planters' Monthly* to fear an "oversupply of this class of immigrants" and consequent loss of control over labor in general.

Coming as they have without women, and under no contracts, save such as binds them helplessly to Chinese organizations, and passing unchecked into our community, is certainly startling. If five thousand come in this noiseless manner, and are not restricted, twenty thousand or more may come. . . . If some . . . plan can be carried out, and only so many Chinese be admitted as we need for laborers, and they be accompanied with their wives, and serve under contracts, and at the termination of their contracts be compelled to return to China unless they enter into new contracts, we would not view Chinese immigration with alarm, but with satisfaction.[11]

The census of 1884, revealing that the "Celestials" constituted 22.6 per cent of the entire population of the Islands and 50.2 per cent of the foreigners, helped to shift public attention and support to other groups, such as the Portuguese and Japanese, as potential laborers and replenishers of Hawaii's population.

Owing to the tendency on the part of many of the unmarried immigrants to return to their homeland after the completion of their plantation contracts, the Chinese population actually declined by approximately 1,500 between 1884 and 1890, but another period of extensive immigration occurring during the nineties resulted in an increase of 9,000 persons, mostly men, before 1900. According to the best estimates, a total of more than 46,000 Chinese were brought to Hawaii as laborers, chiefly between 1876 and 1885 and between 1890 and 1897, and yet only 21,674 persons, including the children born in Hawaii, were enumerated in the census of 1910. With the aid of the Hawaii-born children, the Chinese population increased slowly during the next fifty years, from 21,674 in 1910 to 38,119 in 1960, although their proportion of the total declined from 11.3 per cent to 6 per cent during the same period.

The next major ethnic group to be imported to Hawaii as laborers were physiologically much more closely akin to the planters who brought them to Hawaii, but like the Chinese, they were thought of and treated as a separate racial group as long as they remained on the plantation. Recruited chiefly between 1878 and 1887 from the Azores and Madeira Islands, the 17,500 Portuguese immigrants were con-

[11]*The Planters' Monthly*, May, 1883, p. 25.

2. POPULATION BY RACE, 1853-1960

	1853	1860	1866	1872†	1878†	1884†	1890†	1896†	1900†	1910	1920	1930	1940	1950	1960
NUMBER															
Hawaiian	70,036	65,647	57,125	49,044	44,088	40,014	34,436	31,019	29,799	26,041	23,723	22,636	14,375	12,245	10,502
Part-Hawaiian	983	1,337*	1,640	2,487	3,420	4,218	6,186	8,485	9,857	12,506	18,027	28,224	49,935	73,845	91,597
Caucasian	1,687	1,900†	2,400*	2,944	3,748	16,579	18,939	22,438	26,819	39,158‡	49,140†	73,702‡	103,791§	114,793§	202,230‖
Portuguese	87	85*	90	424	486	9,967	12,719	15,191	18,272	22,301	27,002	27,588			
Other Caucasian	1,600	1,815	2,310	2,520	3,262	6,612	6,220	7,247	8,547	14,867	19,708	44,895			
Chinese	364	816	1,306	2,038	6,045	18,254	16,752	21,616	25,767	21,674	23,507	27,179	28,774	32,376	38,119
Japanese						116	12,610	24,407	61,111	79,675	109,274	139,631	157,905	184,598	203,876
Korean										4,533	4,950	6,461	6,851	7,030	
Filipino										2,361	21,031	63,052	52,569	61,062	68,641
Puerto Rican	5									4,890	5,602	6,671	8,296	9,551	
Negro									233	695	348	563	255	2,651	4,943
All Other	62	100*	488	384	684	1,397	1,067	1,055	415	376	310	217	579	1,618	12,864#
TOTAL	73,137	69,800	62,959	56,897	57,985	80,578	89,990	109,020	154,001	191,909	255,912	368,336	423,330	499,769	632,772
PER CENT OF TOTAL															
Hawaiian	95.8	94.0	90.7	86.2	76.0	49.7	38.2	28.4	19.3	13.6	9.3	6.1	3.4	2.5	1.7
Part-Hawaiian	1.3	1.9	2.6	4.4	5.9	5.2	6.9	7.8	5.1	6.5	7.0	7.7	11.8	14.8	14.5
Caucasian	2.3	2.7	3.8	5.2	6.5	20.6	21.0	20.6	17.3	20.4	19.2	20.0	23.0	23.0	32.0
Portuguese	.1	.1	.1	.7	.8	12.3	14.1	13.9	11.9	11.6	10.6	7.5			
Other Caucasian	2.2	2.6	3.7	4.5	5.7	8.3	6.9	6.7	5.4	7.7	7.7	12.2			
Chinese	.5	1.2	2.0	3.6	10.4	22.6	18.6	19.8	16.7	11.3	9.2	7.4	6.8	6.5	6.0
Japanese						.1	14.0	22.3	39.7	41.5	42.7	37.9	37.3	36.9	32.2
Korean										2.4	1.9	1.8	1.6	1.4	
Filipino										1.2	8.2	17.1	12.4	12.2	10.8
Puerto Rican										2.5	2.2	1.8	2.0	1.9	
Negro									.2	.4	.1	.2	.1	.5	.8
All Other	.1	.1	.8	.7	1.2	1.7	1.2	1.0	.3	.2	.1	.1	.1	.3	2.0

*Estimate. †Based on Romanzo Adams, *The Peoples of Hawaii* (Honolulu: The Institute of Pacific Relations, 1933), pp. 8-9. ‡Includes Spanish, not separately listed. §Includes Spanish and Portuguese, n.s.l. ‖Includes Spanish, Portuguese, and Puerto Ricans, n.s.l. #Includes Koreans, Samoans, Micronesians, n.s.l.

sidered by the planters as a desirable supplement to the Chinese laborers and by the government as effective rebuilders of the declining Hawaiian population. Not only did the Portuguese come to Hawaii with a larger proportion of women than the Chinese, but, partly as a consequence, they were also more disposed to remain as permanent settlers. Characterized by the early promoters of the immigration as a peasant people whose "education and ideas of comfort and social requirements are just low enough to make them contented with the lot of an isolated settler and its attendant privations," [12] the Portuguese were widely acclaimed as likely to solve Hawaii's population problem. In contrast to the womenless Chinese, the Portuguese reproduced rapidly. Although the total number of Chinese imported to Hawaii was more than twice that of Portuguese, by 1910 the Portuguese population had exceeded the Chinese.

Despite the very high cost of bringing the Portuguese to Hawaii by the long trip around Cape Horn and the additional expense of recruiting women and children,[13] the planters and the government of Hawaii continued to experiment with Portuguese immigration during the last decade of the nineteenth and the first two decades of the twentieth centuries. Approximately one quarter of the total immigration of Portuguese occurred between 1906 and 1913,[14] although a considerable number of them were later lost to California.

Owing to the similarities in appearance and culture between the Portuguese and the other Europeans and Americans in Hawaii, there was a distinct disposition for the former to identify with the higher economic and social status of the latter insofar as that was possible. By moving from the plantation to the city and by intermarriage, it was possible for many of the Portuguese to lose their separate identity as a racial group. Although in the census of 1930 there were still 27,588 persons, or 7.5 per cent of the total population, listed as Portuguese, it was decided, probably prematurely, to incorporate that group in the 1940 census with the "Other Caucasians," as will be noted in Figure 1 and Table 2.

The story of Japanese immigration parallels that of the Portuguese in many respects, including the expectation that they would serve to revive the "dying native population." An emissary of the Hawaiian king, seeking to open negotiations with the Japanese government for

[12]Correspondence of the President of the Bureau of Immigration, June 6, 1887, in the Archives of Hawaii, Interior Department File 52.
[13]Required by the Portuguese government as a basis of recruiting laborers for Hawaii. Most of the Portuguese labor immigrants were recruited in the Azores and Madeira Islands.
[14]Adams, *The Peoples of Hawaii*, p. 13.

the importation of laborers to Hawaii, was authorized to state that "His Majesty believes that the Japanese and Hawaiians spring from one cognate race and . . . he hopes our peoples will more and more be brought closer together in a common brotherhood." [15] This belief, however, was apparently not shared by the Japanese. The initial attempt to induce them to migrate to Hawaii in 1868 was carried out in defiance of orders from the government of Japan, with the result that only 148 persons of an expected 350 left the country and no further immigration occurred until 1885.

Following the signing of a convention between Japan and Hawaii in 1886, Japanese peasants began to migrate to the Islands in large numbers for work on the plantations. Thus, although only 116 were listed in the census of 1884, the number of Japanese increased to 12,610 six years later and to 61,111 in 1900. Despite some irritation with the restraints imposed by the Japanese government upon their control of the workers, the planters were evidently pleased with the laborers they had obtained during the first few years of the movement. The *Planters' Monthly* in 1889 reported enthusiastically upon the very small charge of $66.79 for passage money per employee, "all of which is refunded to the employer, so that the actual cost is nothing except the wages paid. No laborers have ever been introduced here on such easy terms. And what is still better, the Japanese readily learn the English language and habits, and make good house, farm, and plantation servants . . . and they are provident and thrifty." [16] This cordiality on the part of both the planters and the general public declined markedly as it became evident that the Japanese might constitute as much of a labor and population threat as the Chinese had a decade earlier. By 1896 the Japanese made up 22.4 per cent of the entire population, and by the turn of the century, nearly 40 per cent was Japanese.

Despite a growing atmosphere of hostility to further immigration, Japanese laborers, to the number of nearly 110,000 within a single decade, were brought into the Territory after Annexation,[17] and women and children continued to arrive until the passage of the Exclusion Act in 1924. This federal legislation, largely in response to pressures from organized labor and small business groups along the

[15]Report of John Kapena's Mission to Japan, November 14, 1882, in Archives of Hawaii, Interior Department File 53.

[16]*The Planters' Monthly*, April 1889, p. 149.

[17]A large number of Japanese, estimated at 40,000, left Hawaii for continental United States in response to the economic opportunities, as well as the greater freedom of movement, which were presumed to exist there. There was at the same time a considerable movement back to Japan.

Pacific Coast, placed an absolute bar upon practically all immigration from Japan, and thus brought to a virtual halt the flow of this largest source of residents from abroad. With Japanese population strength reaching a peak in 1920 when they constituted 42.7 per cent of the total, it is not surprising that myths of a "yellow menace" should also have appeared during that period. With the virtual cessation of further immigration from Japan following the 1924 Exclusion Act, the proportion of Japanese in the total population began to decline, dropping to 37.9 per cent in 1930 and to 32.2 per cent at the time of the 1960 census, and estimates in the mid-sixties by the Department of Planning and Economic Development indicate that it may have declined to less than 30 per cent.

Several of the smaller ethnic groups were introduced in the decade following Annexation, partly as foils to the large Japanese population. Nearly 6,000 Puerto Ricans arrived chiefly in 1901, about 8,000 Koreans in 1904 and 1905, while an equal number of Spaniards were recruited in the years 1907 to 1913. So great was the emigration of the Spaniards to California that there were never more than 2,430 recorded by the census (in 1920), and since 1930 they have ceased to figure at all as a separate group in the census. The Puerto Ricans, on the other hand, have remained and reproduced within the Islands. Despite the fact that they were initially the smallest of these three immigrant groups, they now have the largest population, although this statement cannot be statistically verified owing to the lack of census reporting for these groups. The Koreans numbered only 7,030 in 1950 when they were last separately enumerated in the census, a count which was less than the total number of their immigrants to Hawaii in the first decade of the present century.

The Filipinos were the last of the major ethnic groups to enter the Territory, nearly 120,000 being imported as plantation laborers during the period from 1907 to 1931. By the time the Filipinos appeared on the Hawaiian scene, it was no longer necessary to justify the importation on the grounds of solving a population problem. The disastrous effects of the 1909 strike gave the planters good reason to seek relief from the near monopoly of plantation labor by the Japanese. Economic considerations were foremost in the recruiting of Filipino immigrants as is suggested by the extreme disproportion of males to females which exceeded four to one during most of the early period and ran as high as nineteen to one during the years from 1924 to 1930. A supplementary importation of about 6,000 male workers and some 3,000 women and children occurred in July 1946 to ease the plantation labor shortage created by World War II.

The proportion of Filipinos to the total population of the Islands reached a peak of 17.1 per cent in 1930, and because of the extensive movement of the single men back to the Philippines or to California, the number of Filipinos left in Hawaii declined by 11,000 in the decade 1930-1940. The Filipinos constituted slightly less than one out of eight in the population at the 1940 and 1950 census enumerations, and even this number included in 1950 some 7,680 persons of mixed ancestry. In 1960, there was a total of 69,070 persons classified as Filipino, constituting 10.9 per cent of the total.

The positions of power and prestige enjoyed by most of the Haoles, almost from the first arrival of Captain Cook, has accorded them, at least until the outbreak of World War II, a markedly different experience in Hawaii from that of the other immigrant groups thus far considered. Whether as the early tradesmen who could supply the natives with the foreign artifacts they eagerly sought, or as missionaries who taught and advised on all matters relating to the new way of life, or as the planters and promoters of the new economy, throughout the first century and a half of contact the Haoles expected and, for the most part, received a status superior to that of most natives and of all the immigrant labor groups.

The proportion of the population who could occupy such positions of influence and prestige was necessarily limited, and no large numbers of Haoles were reported in the censuses throughout the nineteenth century. During most of the period of rapid plantation development (1876-1930), the Haoles or "Other Caucasians," as they were classified in the U. S. Census reports after Annexation, did not keep numerical pace with the rest of the population, dropping from 8.3 per cent in 1884 to 5.4 per cent in 1900. Even in the two succeeding decades there was only a slight increase in the proportion of Haoles, and it was not until Hawaii began to figure prominently as a military and tourist frontier that their numbers and their proportion of the total population rose markedly. Although separate census figures for the Haoles as separate from the Caucasians have not been available since 1930, the Haole proportion had risen to 12.2 per cent at that time, and by 1960 it was probably close to 25 per cent.

AGE AND SEX

A region populated so largely by immigrants and immigrant children is bound to be profoundly affected by the age and sex composition of its peoples. The long and sometimes arduous voyages necessary to carry the early immigrants to Hawaii quite naturally drew more heavily upon the young and active than upon the aged and decrepit, and in most groups it was the males more than the females who did the pioneering. The permanence and the survival of the groups are determined, however, by a different set of factors than those which initiate the migrations. It is a frequently over-looked truism that only women of certain ages bear children, and the extent of their presence in a population is a critical factor in determining the survival of the group.

The existence, moreover, of any large number of single adult males without the presence of a corresponding female population is bound to have profound consequences upon the moral tone of the community. This is as true of the plantation camps or the military installations of Hawaii as it is of the pioneer mining, lumbering, or fishing communities of the American West, Alaska, or South Africa. The notion that there is neither God nor law on the frontier is doubt-less an exaggeration, but neither God nor law can be as readily recognized there as in the community with a more normal age and sex distribution.

Especially in the period since the rapid expansion of plantation enterprise and of extensive immigration, Hawaii's population has shown a considerable excess of men over women and an essentially youthful appearance. Even in 1853 there was the fairly pronounced sex differential of 113 males to every 100 females in the total population. As one would expect, this differential was most apparent among the immigrant groups, with 447 males to every 100 females. The excess of 9.5 males to every 100 females among the native Hawaiians is probably attributable to the practice of female in-fanticide, which still persisted to some degree and which continued to manifest itself in census returns until after the turn of the century. The maximum sex differential among the natives appears to have been reached about 1884 with a ratio of 116.2 males per 100 females, and an equal proportion between the sexes was not reached until 1930.

One of the most effective devices for reflecting changes in both the age and sex distributions of any population is the simple graph known as the population pyramid, the left half of which indicates the age distribution of the males, while the right represents the females. The population of a region unaffected by migration tends to assume the form of an isosceles triangle, with approximately equal proportions of males and females on the left and right sides and

1920   1960

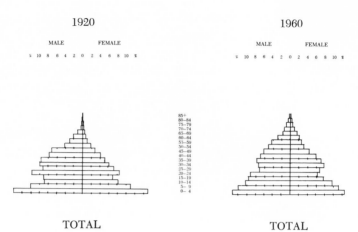

TOTAL   TOTAL

HAWAIIAN   HAWAIIAN
(Including PH)   (Including PH)

   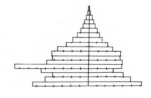

CAUCASIAN   CAUCASIAN

Figure 2. Age and Sex Pyramids

1920   1960

CHINESE   CHINESE

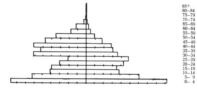

JAPANESE   JAPANESE

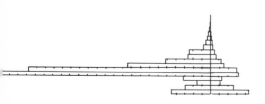

FILIPINO   FILIPINO

a gradual decline in numbers from the base to the vertex according to age. In a stationary population, losses through death in the upper age levels are balanced by births at the base of the pyramid. To indicate the changing age and sex structure of the major ethnic groups of the Islands, population pyramids for 1920 and 1960 are presented in Figures 2a and 2b.

The combined Hawaiian and Part-Hawaiian pyramids most nearly approximate a normal distribution, with, however, a decidedly broad base in 1920 and an even slightly broader one in 1960. The median age of 16.0 years for the Hawaiian males was lower than that of any other major ethnic group in Hawaii in 1960, and only the Filipino women had as low a median age as that of the Hawaiian females (16.8 years). The Hawaiians give no evidence in their population pyramid of any disposition during the first half of the twentieth century to restrict births as a means of attaining a higher plane of living.

The Chinese provide perhaps the most striking example of a group whose immigrant population abnormalities have largely disappeared. In 1920 more than 36 per cent of the Chinese in Hawaii were middle-aged and elderly men, between the ages of 35 and 64, the remnants of the immigration which had ceased some twenty years earlier. By 1960 this remnant had all but disappeared, with only a slight excess of males over the age of 80. Contrast this with the experience of the Filipinos—in 1920 more than 56 per cent were young men between the ages of 20 and 34, and there was less than one woman to every seven men. The abnormalities in the age and sex distributions among the Filipinos were much less pronounced in 1960, but the disproportion between the sexes was still strikingly high in the middle and older age levels. Even in the 40- to 44-year grouping, the ratio of males to females was somewhat more than two to one, and among those aged 45 to 54 years there was only one woman to every 6.5 men. The striking contrast in 1960 between the median age of Filipino males (38.6 years) and of Filipino females (16.8 years), which is without parallel in any other ethnic group in the Islands, highlights one of the major social problems in the Islands. When one considers that less than one out of every three Filipino men aged 45 years and over was married and living with his wife in 1960 and that the great majority of Filipino men had been denied normal family associations and sex relations for thirty or more of the most vigorous years of life, it is not particularly surprising that in certain forms of mental breakdown, sex delinquencies, and crimes of violence and passion, their rates are above average.

Because the Japanese immigrants came to Hawaii more generously provided with women than either the Chinese or Filipinos, the disproportions in the sex ratios have never been so apparent. At the peak of the plantation era, in 1920, the immigrant Japanese were largely in the 30- to 54-year age bracket, within which the males rarely exceeded the females by more than two to one. By 1960 only a few of the immigrant generation remained in the age class of 60 years and over, within which there was still some evidence of an excess of males over females.

The effects of the competitive struggle for status and for a higher plane of living during the pre-war period are reflected in the clearly marked underproportion in 1960 of persons aged 20 to 34, especially among the Chinese and Japanese. This same trend was noted ten years earlier among those aged 10 to 24. Here is evidence of the declining birth rate during the two decades preceding the war, while the post-war baby-boom and the mounting economic affluence in the 1950's is reflected in the higher proportions of children, especially under the age of fifteen. The somewhat temporary nature of the post-war population explosion is suggested in these two ethnic groups by the reduced proportion of population under the age of five in 1960. Quite obviously the Hawaiians and the Filipinos have not responded to these forces in the same way as the Chinese and Japanese, or else there have been other important influences operating on them. Of the smaller groups not represented in Figure 2 but for whom census data were available in 1950, the Koreans had at that time an age and sex structure during the first forty years of life which roughly paralleled that of the Chinese or Japanese, while the age and sex structure among the Puerto Ricans more nearly approximated that of the Filipinos.

The population pyramids for the Caucasians are somewhat less revealing than the others due to the composite character of that group. The combination of the Portuguese and "Other Caucasian" groups tends to disguise somewhat the real situation. The Portuguese group alone had an age and sex distribution in 1920 strikingly similar to that of the combined Hawaiian population—an equal ratio between the sexes and a disproportionately high ratio of children. The Other Caucasians, on the other hand, had a very narrow base and a high proportion of males in the late teens, the twenties, thirties, and extending into the forties. The excess of males over females in the early years of maturity, amounting to approximately three males to every female in 1920, was a consequence of the growing military frontier in Hawaii, and this disparity became even more acute in 1930 and 1940. Even in the pyramid for the combined Caucasian group in 1960 the presence of more than twice as many men as women between the ages of 15 and 24 is a clear reminder that Hawaii is still a military frontier. Overproportions of males at all other ages under 65 probably reflect the influence of a combination of the military, plantation, and commercial frontiers in Hawaii.

3

WHERE DO THEY LIVE?

A LAND OF MANY ISLANDS

Equally as important as the fact that Hawaii's people all live some two thousand miles from their nearest continental neighbors is the fact of their separation from one another on the eight major islands of the group and the far more numerous land islands, created by high mountains, steep palis, and deep valleys. Hawaii is not a flat plain over which the population might flow in one contiguous and homogeneous mass. Hawaii is, by its volcanic character, a host of little islands, each of which might provide the home for a separate and distinct cultural world. Not only every island, as Robert E. Park observed, but every major subdivision within the eight islands of the group may enclose

not merely another community but a different world, each with its own local traditions and way of life, and each more or less self-sufficing and complete in itself. Possibly these differences are not actually as great as they seem but the effect of isolation, which life on an island imposes, is to intensify personal intimacies, and by so doing promotes the growth of local customs in response to local conditions. Insularity, in short, encourages individuality and in this sense, it is true that one cannot tell what will happen on an island.[1]

Park's description of the Island scene is particularly appropriate for the pre-European and frontier periods of Hawaiian history, but it is also valid to a considerable degree even at the present time.

The shifting population of Hawaii has been scattered over eight major islands, making up a land mass of only 6,412 square miles

[1] Robert E. Park in the Introduction of Romanzo Adams, *Interracial Marriage in Hawaii* (New York: The Macmillan Company, 1937), pp. xii.

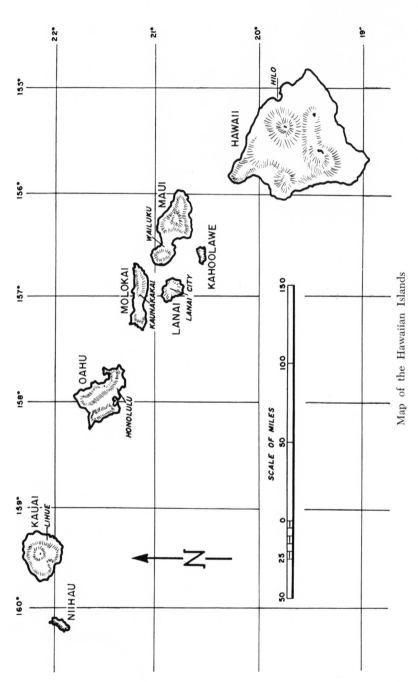

Map of the Hawaiian Islands

of territory—roughly equal to the area of the state of New Jersey. Seven of the eight islands strewn along a four-hundred-mile arc have been continuously inhabited since prehistoric times. The five largest in order of area—Hawaii, Maui, Oahu, Kauai, and Molokai— have always had a population in excess of a thousand each during the period for which we have accurate information. The sixth and seventh in area—Lanai and Niihau, with land areas of 141 and 72 squares miles respectively—during most of the last hundred years have supported populations of only a few hundred each. The remaining major island, Kahoolawe, and even the more important minor islands such as Lehua, Kaula, Palmyra, and the leeward group, have appeared only sporadically in census returns.

The populations supported by these different land masses have varied greatly from one another under both the native and the Western conditions of life. Hawaii, the largest and geologically the youngest of the islands, has probably never had a permanent population of much more than 73,325, recorded in 1930. The Big Island's extensive land area of 4,021 square miles, which is considerably more than the whole of Puerto Rico with its nearly two and a half million inhabitants, has always had vast areas virtually devoid of human population.

The extensive lava wastes and huge mountain domes rising almost 14,000 feet above sea level divide the island mass into at least six major districts, which were sometimes the bases of separate kingdoms during the pre-European era. The drop in the population of the island from the figure of 45,679 [2] reported in the first missionary census (1831-32) to a low of 16,001 in 1872 left vast areas uninhabited, but even the maximum population recorded under modern times would give the island a density of only 18.3 persons per square mile as compared with 98.6 for the entire state and of 50.5 for the entire United States in 1960. The downward trend in population from 73,325 in 1930 to 61,332 in 1960 is slowly being reversed with the growth in the tourist industry, but, considering the recent volcanic character of the island, there are bound to be large unpopulated areas. There are vast sections of potentially arable land still unoccupied, the development of which will present a challenge to human ingenuity for many years to come.

With the exception of Oahu, the other larger islands of the group—Maui, Lanai, Molokai, and Kauai—have followed much the

[2]Captain King's estimate of 150,000 inhabitants in 1779 was unquestionably too high. Cf. Adams, *Interracial Marriage in Hawaii*, pp. 1-2.

same pattern of population change as Hawaii. Their people have been supported almost wholly by the land, and the numbers have therefore fluctuated according to the changing balance between man and his sources of livelihood. During the first century of contact with the Western world, man's biological enemies, in the form of numerous new disease germs, were in the ascendancy, and the native population declined on all the islands, first very rapidly and then more slowly. With the rise of the plantations, as a new element in the biological balance of the Islands, new peoples were introduced from outside and the downward trend in population was reversed. This occurred on all the islands at about the same time—just after the Reciprocity Treaty of 1876 went into effect.

Then, as a consequence of the expanding plantation economy, the population of all the islands increased rapidly over a period of somewhat more than fifty years. The four major islands on which the plantation economy was concentrated—Hawaii, Maui, Oahu, and Kauai—all increased in population more rapidly during the fifty years following 1878 than they had declined during the previous forty-five years. Between 1930 and 1960, with the passing of the peak of plantation domination and the corresponding technological changes within the plantations, there was again a decline of population on all the major islands except Oahu. The expansion of the tourist industry has brought about some slight increase in population on Maui, Kauai, and Hawaii during the middle sixties, and this trend will doubtless continue.

Oahu alone continued to increase in population throughout the period since 1853. Owing chiefly to its central position with reference to the other islands and the excellence of its Honolulu and Pearl harbors, Oahu began early to attract visitors and settlers who were engaged primarily in trade. Even in 1853, Honolulu district had a disproportionate share of the population of the Islands—11,455 as compared with 7,748 in the entire Hilo and Puna districts on Hawaii, Honolulu's closest competitors. By 1872, Oahu had outstripped all the other islands, and by the early 1920's more than half of the residents of the entire Territory lived on Oahu.

Honolulu's function as the controlling center of the plantation enterprises and as the political capital of the Islands was chiefly responsible for the striking growth in population on Oahu prior to 1930. Since that date, the number of residents on Oahu has continued to increase with equally startling rapidity, chiefly as a consequence of its military and commercial functions in the Pacific. It comes as something of a shock to those who have thought of Hawaii as a sub-tropical agricultural region to discover that in 1960 more than 79 per cent of the residents were located on one island with less than 10 per cent of the total land area and that well over half (55.5 per cent) of the residents of the state lived in the city of Honolulu or its adjacent urbanized area. In every census since 1853 Oahu has outstripped all the neighboring islands in population density.

It is not commonly recognized that the major agricultural enterprises in Hawaii have been highly industrialized and that, to a far greater degree than in most other plantation frontiers of the world, the persons engaged in cultivating and processing such crops as sugar cane and pineapples in Hawaii live within the orbit of the city and enjoy whatever material and cultural advantages it has to offer.[3] Thus it develops that more than three-quarters (76.5 per cent) of the residents of the state in 1960 were classified by the census as urban, in contrast with 69.9 per cent of the residents of continental United States as a whole. In comparison to 1920 when there were twenty-two of today's fifty states with a higher proportion of their people living in urban centers, in 1960 there were only seven—Massachusetts, Connecticut, Rhode Island, New York, New Jersey, Illinois, and California. In contrast with 86.5 per cent of Oahu's population in urban areas, on the other larger islands, 49.5 per cent on Maui, 42.3 per cent on Hawaii, and 26.3 on Kauai were classified as urban, but these are still significantly high for areas in which income is derived almost wholly from agriculture.

In contrast to the clearly defined population trends in the plantation areas before 1930 and the strong cityward movement on Oahu, there have been a number of remote districts on all of the islands in which the population has remained relatively stable for the greater part of the past century. These are the areas, to be discussed in the next section, where native culture has retained its strongest foothold. Most striking of such areas is the island of Niihau on whose 72 square miles barely two hundred persons on an average have found a livelihood for the past eighty years. Since 1872 the island has continued to report about the same number of residents—slightly below 200 at most of the census periods, dropping to a low of 136 in 1930 and increasing to 254 in 1960. Molokai, despite its partial development for the cultivation of plantation crops, also retains an essentially rural atmosphere and its characterization as the "Lonely Island" is still somewhat justi-

---

[3] Andrew W. Lind, *An Island Community* (Chicago: University of Chicago Press, 1938), pp. 298-304.

3. AREA AND POPULATION BY ISLANDS, 1853-1960

	Land Area (sq. mi.)	Population					Per Cent of Total					Density 1960 (per sq. mi.)
		1853	1878	1930	1950	1960	1853	1878	1930	1950	1960	
Hawaii	4,021	24,450	17,034	73,325	68,350	61,332	33.4	29.4	19.9	13.7	9.7	15.3
Kahoolawe	45											
Maui	728	17,574	12,109	48,758	40,103	35,717	24.0	20.9	13.2	8.0	5.6	49.1
Lanai	141	600	214	2,356	3,136	2,115	.8	.4	.6	.6	.3	15.0
Molokai	259	3,607	2,581	5,032	5,280	5,023	5.0	4.4	1.4	1.0	.7	19.4
Oahu	598	19,126	20,236	202,887	353,020	500,409	26.2	34.9	55.1	70.6	79.1	836.8
Kauai	551	6,991	5,634	35,806	29,683	27,922	9.6	9.7	9.7	5.9	4.4	50.7
Niihau	72	790	177	136	222	254	1.0	.3	.1	.2	.2	3.5
TOTAL	6,415	73,138	57,985	368,300	499,794	632,772	100.0	100.0	100.0	100.0	100.0	98.6

fied. Of the forty-four major geographical subdivisions recognized by the census in 1960, fifteen, including North and South Kohala, North Kona, and North Hilo on the Big Island, Haiku, Hana, Kihei, Kula, and Waihee on Maui, the three districts of Molokai, Hanalei and Hanamaulu districts on Kauai, and Niihau, had no communities exceeding a thousand inhabitants.

THE HABITAT OF THE HAWAIIANS

As one would expect, Hawaiian culture and population have persisted most effectively in areas where Western civilization has penetrated least. Thus census reports from 1853 to 1960 reveal that the islands and districts least suitable for plantation agriculture or other Western uses have remained the havens for native Hawaiians. A century ago the native population was still dominant in every island district from Puna to Niihau. The two remote islands of Lanai and Niihau, with 600 and 790 Hawaiians respectively, had not a single foreigner or Part-Hawaiian resident. Of the larger islands, Hawaii, with its vast lava wastes and huge mountain domes, had been affected least by foreign contacts, and only 1.1 per cent of its population was non-Hawaiian. The three districts of Puna, Kau, and South Kona on the southern half of the island noted for the large area of barren lava flows supported a native population of 8,040, but only 45 foreigners. Nearly a third of the 17,330 natives on the neighboring island of Maui were residents of isolated Hana, to which only 10 of the 244 foreigners on the island had been attracted.

In 1853, the largest numbers of foreigners had settled on the islands of Oahu and Kauai, but both had their isolated districts also where native culture was able to survive to a considerable degree. Although the population of Honolulu district was one-tenth foreign, across the Pali were two districts of 4,054 natives, with only 1 per cent foreigners. In the Waimea district of Kauai—remote from the major ports—were resident 30 per cent of the native population and only 7 per cent of the foreign population of the entire island.

The expansion of the plantations during the last half of the nineteenth century reduced considerably the area within which the Hawaiians could maintain some numerical and cultural dominance, but the lonely islands of Niihau, Lanai, and Molokai remained relatively free of foreign influence until well after Annexation. In 1930 there were seventeen remote districts in which the Hawaiians constituted more than 50 per cent of the population. These were:

the dry and rocky portions of Kau, Puna, and the deep valley of Waipio (on Hawaii), the wild sections of Hana, Maui, portions of Lanai and Molokai where industrial methods of agriculture have not succeeded, the leper settlement, and Niihau, the island of mystery . . . the places of refuge for some 4,400, or nearly one-fifth, of the native Polynesians. Scores of smaller valleys and isolated districts scattered over the Islands—too small or too barren to attract any numbers of the foreign population and therefore too insignificant to appear as separate enumeration districts—provide havens for a few families of the old Hawaiians.

The old fish and poi economy, with its accompaniment of tutelary deities, tabus, religion and magic, still persists in modified form within many of these isolated communities. A small plot of taro and access to the sea and the mountains are apparently all that is required for the satisfaction of their material wants. The wage from an occasional day's work on the government road enables them to purchase the necessary supplies which the old economy cannot now provide. Except in Molokai, where sequestration of lepers has brought a disproportionately large number of natives, no governmental paternalism has occasioned this racial segregation in Hawaii. The natives themselves have found these rural havens where the economy of life to which they are best adapted can survive.[4]

That the situation had not been seriously altered by 1950 is reflected in the reports of ten census tracts in which the Hawaiians constituted more than 50 per cent of the residents and of eight additional tracts in which they were the largest racial group. These centers of Hawaiian concentration were in the economically retarded and remote sections of Kohala, Kona, Kalapana, and Kau on the Big Island, of Hana and Waihee on Maui, of East Molokai, of Koolauloa on Oahu, and the island of Niihau. Although the 1960 census did not provide similar data, except on Oahu, a clearly disproportionate ratio of Hawaiians in all the larger census divisions of which they are a part would indicate that the rural native havens still remain.

Included within these areas are first of all the small subsistence communities, such as Kalapana, Milolii, Hookena, Honaunau, Napoopoo, Waipio, Keanae, and Pukoo, where small numbers of Hawaiians continue to derive much of their livelihood as their ancestors did generations ago—from the sea and the soil immediately—but supplemented by income from the sale of fish or taro or by occasional work on county roads or for the invading tourists and movie promoters. The number involved in such communities is necessarily small, probably not exceeding two thousand in the aggregate but nevertheless representing areas of special interest to social scientists.

The second rural community in which Hawaiians assume a dominant position are the cattle ranches, which by their nature are situated in the remote, mountainous, and least suitable agricultural lands.

[4]*Ibid.*, pp. 102-103.

Communities such as Kamuela and the outlying portions of Kona on Hawaii, Hana on Maui, and the island of Niihau come immediately to mind as areas in which Hawaiian cowboys and ranch hands predominate, although on all the islands numerous other smaller communities exist in which ranching is conducted in conjunction with small scale agriculture or the plantations. There is, incidentally, considerable similarity in the paternalistic structure of both the ranch and the early plantation with, however, a greater degree of freedom of action and movement to appeal especially to Hawaiians on the cattle ranches.

More important in the total experience of the natives than the survival of a few thousand persons in these isolated pockets on the edges of the expanding Western world has been the gradual absorption of the Hawaiians into the more centrally situated aspects of this evolving community. Each new census has told the story of a larger proportion who have been drawn within the orbit of the commercial economy, centering in the port towns and cities.

Of the numerous native villages scattered along the coastline of the several islands—where the early trading and exploring vessels might obtain food and refreshment—Honolulu soon emerged as the dominant center. The harbor first came to the attention of the visiting Westerners in 1794, but natives had clearly made use of the rich lands and fishing grounds much earlier. The possibilities of gainful exchange at this site soon attracted haole traders and natives alike, so that by 1821 an estimated 3,000 had concentrated in a "straggling village." Ten years later the first missionary census reported a village of "5,522 inhabitants, including 180 foreigners." [5]

The Hawaiian censuses from 1853 to 1896 do not report the population of Honolulu city separately from the district (Maunalua to Moanalua), but it appears that as the century advanced, the Honolulu district consistently drew a higher proportion of the total Hawaiian population of the Islands. Thus, between 1853 and 1900, the total native population dropped from 71,019 to 29,799, while the native population resident in Honolulu district declined only from 10,275 to 8,385. During the same period of time, the proportion of all the pure Hawaiians in the Islands who were resident in Honolulu increased from 14.5 per cent to 28.1 per cent. The same pull of the large city on the native Hawaiians continued during the first half of the twentieth century, so that in 1950 slightly more than 40 per cent

---

[5] "Extracts from the Journal of Mr. Bingham at Honolulu," *The Missionary Herald,* XXVIII, No. 11 (November, 1832), 353.

of the reported twelve thousand "pure" Hawaiians lived in Honolulu. The same trend was even more evident among the Part-Hawaiians, of whose small number in the total population a disproportionate 40 per cent were enumerated in the Honolulu district, and, as compared with both the pure Hawaiians and the total population, the Part-Hawaiians have continued to report a higher proportion in the capital city down to 1950. The tendency for Part-Hawaiians to be born or to gravitate to the towns and cities to a greater degree than the full-blooded natives is consistent with the experience in other parts of the world.[6]

A curious reversal of the earlier cityward trend among the two Hawaiian groups appears to have taken place during the decade following 1950, since the proportion of both full and Part-Hawaiians who were resident in Honolulu dropped between 1950 and 1960. On the other hand, the proportion of both groups which is resident on the Island of Oahu has continued to increase steadily until 1960, suggesting that the attraction of the city still operates but that there is a preference for the suburban and peripheral areas outside the city proper. Sections along the sea shore of Oahu, such as Waimanalo, Heeia, Waikane, Kaaawa, Hauula, Waianae, and Nanakuli, which have thus far not been preempted for other uses, show a disproportionately high ratio of Hawaiians and Part-Hawaiians, but all of these small communities are within an hour's driving time of Honolulu.

The creation of homesteading sites for the special benefit of Hawaiians has paradoxically had the effect of assisting this urban trend rather than the "return to the soil" which the Congressional legislation in 1920 was designed to encourage.

The Hawaiian Homes Commission Act of 1920 was avowedly designed to contribute to the "rehabilitation" of those members of the community with 50 per cent or more Hawaiian blood. . . . By facilitating the return of these people to agricultural pursuits, and especially the development of family farms, it was contended that the Act would promote a more health-ful life, an increase in the numbers of the Hawaiian "race," and a more successful adjustment to the dominant westernized society, without entail-ing the loss of ethnic identity.[7]

The communities founded under the act have been artificially created for persons of Hawaiian ancestry, conceiving of them more or less as wards of the state, or at least as deserving of special consideration from the state. It is significant, however, that of the total of 1,752

[6] R. E. Park, "Race Relations and Certain Frontiers," in E. B. Reuter, ed., *Race and Culture Contacts* (New York: McGraw-Hill, 1934), p. 73.
[7] Allan A. Spitz, *Social Aspects of the Hawaiian Homes Program* (Honolulu: Legislative Reference Bureau, 1964), p. 1.

homesteads in 1964, over half (961) were on the Island of Oahu, 321 in Honolulu proper (Papakolea), 257 at Waimanalo, and 387 at Nanakuli, and that the "more than 1500 applications for leases on file with the department (are) primarily for homesteads on Oahu." [8]

THE CHANGING HABITAT OF OTHER ISLANDERS

In contrast with the Hawaiians and Part-Hawaiians, the immigrant labor groups have gravitated chiefly to either the plantations or the cities and towns, with a limited number of intermediate movements to small farming areas or to military or tourist centers. With the plantations chiefly responsible for their introduction to the islands, the workers almost without exception found in the camps in the midst of the cane or pineapple fields their initial and sometimes their permanent places of residence in Hawaii, but most of them have also utilized the city as another area of adjustment to Island life.

The Chinese and the Portuguese, the labor immigrant groups first to arrive in Hawaii, illustrate two contrasting modes of fitting into the Island community. These are reflected in the speed with which the two groups have shifted their residence from the plantation to the cities and towns. The Chinese have spent a minimum of time in the areas of first settlement, whereas the Portuguese have been much slower in leaving the plantations for an urban environment. In 1884, for example, the outlines of the emerging industrialized agriculture of the Kingdom could be traced by the areas or districts in which a sizeable proportion of Chinese and Portuguese were reported in the census. Thus on Hawaii, each of the districts of Hilo, Hamakua, North Kohala, and Kau had populations of 400 or more of both Chinese and Portuguese, while the remaining districts of Puna, North and South Kona, and South Kohala had less than sixty of each group. Already, however, 29.1 per cent of all the Chinese in the Islands were established in Honolulu, as compared with only 6.2 per cent of the Portuguese and 25.4 of the total population.

In succeeding censuses the difference in the urbanization of the two groups became more marked. In 1930, the last date for which accurate comparable figures are available, 44.6 per cent of the Portuguese in contrast to 71.2 per cent of the Chinese were resident in Honolulu. The pull of the plantation on the Portuguese in 1930 is reflected in their over-representation on the Hilo coast of the Big Island and in the Wailuku and Makawao areas of Maui. The very sharp urban trend of the Chinese population continued through 1950 when

[8]*Ibid.*, p. 12.

4. POPULATION IN HONOLULU BY RACE, 1853-1960

	Honolulu Population					Per Cent of Hawaii Total				
	1853	1896	1920	1950	1960	1853	1896	1920	1950	1960
Hawaiian	9,889	7,918	8,459	4,885	3,828	14.2	25.5	35.7	40.0	36.4
Part-Hawaiian	386	3,468	9,072	37,205	40,749	39.3	40.9	50.3	50.4	44.5
Caucasian	1,013	8,041	23,284	58,555	80,274	60.0	35.8	47.4	51.0	39.7
Portuguese	32	3,833	9,978	†	†	36.8	25.2	37.0	†	†
*Other Caucasian**	981	4,208	13,306	†	†	61.3	58.1	60.1	†	†
Chinese	124	7,693	13,383	26,724	30,078	34.1	35.6	56.9	82.5	78.9
Japanese		2,381	24,522	92,510	109,066		9.8	22.4	50.1	53.5
Korean			1,319	4,802	‡			26.7	68.3	‡
Filipino	3		2,113	17,372	21,807	60.0		10.0	28.5	31.8
Puerto Rican			841	3,904	†			15.0	40.9	†
Others	40	419	334	2,050	8,392	64.5	39.7	50.7	48.0	47.1
TOTAL	11,455	29,920	83,327	248,007	294,194	15.7	27.4	32.6	49.6	46.5

*Includes Spanish.
†Included in Caucasian.
‡Included in Others.

82.5 per cent were resident in Honolulu as compared with 49.6 per cent of the total population. When account is taken of the residents in all communities with a population of 2,500 persons or more, it appears that 91.7 per cent of all Chinese in Hawaii in 1950 were urbanized. The census returns for 1960 would seem to indicate a drop in the proportion of Chinese living in Honolulu proper, but the ratio living in all urban areas, including that adjacent to Honolulu, had increased to the unparalleled high of 94.4 per cent. Thus, although both groups have been attracted by the opportunities of the city, the Chinese, with their stronger commercial tradition, have responded much more readily than the Portuguese. It might almost be said of the Portuguese during the period since 1930 that they had been less urbanized than assimilated, having disappeared as a separate ethnic group in most census counts and official statistics, except in the rural areas.

The other ethnic groups have tended to follow one or the other of these two patterns of community adjustment or some variant of them. The Koreans particularly have found the city a suitable area of settlement, and considering the recency of their arrival, the proportion of their population in Honolulu is almost as high as that of the Chinese. The Puerto Ricans, on the other hand, have roughly paralleled the Portuguese in respect to urbanization. Although the Puerto Ricans arrived on the Hawaiian plantations at about the same time as the Koreans, only 15 per cent of their population had established themselves in Honolulu by 1920, as compared with 26.7 per cent of the Koreans. Much the same difference existed in 1950 when the proportion of the Puerto Ricans living in Honolulu was 40.9 per cent, in contrast with 68.3 per cent of the Koreans. The only other point of heavy concentration of Koreans was the city of Wahiawa, where an additional 9.8 per cent of the population resided, securing their livelihood chiefly from serving the personnel of the neighboring military installation at Schofield Barracks. The Puerto Ricans, on the other hand, have continued to live to a large extent in the plantation and rural farm areas of Hawaii, Maui, and Kauai.

The Filipinos have moved into Honolulu from the plantations at about the same rate as the Puerto Ricans, with a somewhat more rapid rate of urbanization during World War II and just afterwards. In 1940, roughly ten years after the close of Filipino immigration to Hawaii and fifteen or more years after the arrival of most of them, only 13 per cent of all the Filipinos were living in Honolulu. By 1950, however, even with the addition of some 7,361 immigrants in 1946, 28.5 per cent of the Filipinos had settled in the capital city, and slightly more than half of all the Filipinos were classified as urban, i.e., as living in communities with populations of 2,500 or more. A decade later the proportion of the Filipinos living in all urban areas of the state had increased to 63.1 per cent and in Honolulu, to 31.8 per cent, but they were still markedly over-represented in all the plantation districts of the Islands.

The Japanese have been less rapidly urbanized than either the Chinese or the Koreans, but considering their length of residence in Hawaii, they have responded to the pull of the city more readily than the Portuguese, Puerto Ricans, or Filipinos. During the twenty years of their active recruitment as laborers for the plantations (1886-1907), the Japanese were overwhelmingly a rural population. A sizeable minority of 6,179 persons, or slightly more than 10 per cent of their total number, were already residents of Honolulu in 1900, and by 1920 the Japanese population in Honolulu had increased to 24,522, or 22.4 per cent of their entire population in the Territory. According to the 1960 census, the residents of Japanese ancestry in Honolulu numbered 109,066, constituting in themselves a good-sized city, and their proportion of the population of the city (37 per cent) was, like that of the Chinese and Part-Hawaiians, higher than their proportion in the entire state. In part because of their greater identification with the plantations in adjacent areas, the Japanese have been attracted to the smaller cities and towns in somewhat greater proportions than the other ethnic groups. For example, in Hilo, the second largest city of the state, the Japanese numbered 12,193 in 1960, or 47 per cent of the total. Similarly in such plantation-oriented towns as Wahiawa, Waipahu, Wailuku, Honokaa, Lahaina, and Lihue, the Japanese have been disproportionately represented during the past thirty years.

Along with the cityward trend of the Japanese, there has also been a distinct movement on the part of some toward the non-plantation farming areas such as Kona, Kamuela, and the volcano area on the Big Island and the Kula district on Maui. In these and smaller areas on the other islands, it has been possible for sizeable numbers of both first and second generation Japanese to enjoy a greater degree of independence than on the plantations and at the same time to continue a traditional mode of life, somewhat protected from the highly competitive and morally disintegrating influences of the city. For every census period since 1910 for which such data have been available, the Japanese have constituted a significantly disproportionate number of the farm operators in the Islands. The over-representation of Japanese, with ratios of 40-43 per cent on the three islands of

Hawaii, Maui, and Kauai in which agriculture is the principal source of income, was still clearly observable in 1960, although less markedly so than a decade earlier.

The experience of the Haoles in finding homes in the Islands has been quite different from that of either the native Hawaiians or of the immigrant labor groups just described. As the first invaders and the promoters of both commercial and plantation enterprises in the Islands, the Haoles were able to set the stage for the movements of the other groups, including the Hawaiians. Of the sixteen hundred Haoles living in Hawaii in 1853, nearly two-thirds had established themselves in Honolulu, with smaller settlements in the port towns of Lahaina, Hilo, and Kahului, and a small scattering elsewhere in the Islands. There were no Haoles registered on either Lanai or Niihau and only 43 on the whole of Molokai.

The influence of the Haoles in the establishment and prosecution of plantation enterprises is by no means reflected in their numbers in the plantation areas. In 1896, for example, Honolulu still claimed nearly 60 per cent of all the Haoles in Hawaii, and throughout the other major districts of all the islands except Lihue, Kauai, where the German plantation laborers were included, they were under-represented. Even in 1930, which was the last census in which there was a separate listing of Other Caucasians or Haoles, 53.5 per cent of them resided in Honolulu. In the meantime, however, Hawaii had become an important military outpost of the United States, with the result that another quarter of the Haole population was settled in the Wahiawa (Schofield Barracks) district of Oahu. Sizeable haole populations were also living in the port cities of the other islands, and there were small compact settlements of haole managers and technical personnel on all of the plantations.

The practice of combining Haoles and Portuguese in the subsequent censuses prevents accurate comparisons, but in 1960 the combined Caucasian group was still disproportionately represented on the Island of Oahu, but especially in the areas outside of Honolulu, where they constituted 48 per cent of the total population. The Caucasian military personnel in the Hickam-Pearl Harbor, Schofield Barracks, and Kaneohe districts, plus the civilian and military residents of Honolulu and its suburbs, accounted for 88.5 per cent of the Caucasian population of the state in 1960.

ISLANDS WITHIN THE CITY

Every large city in the Western world tends to act somewhat like a sieve, sifting and sorting its population and institutions according to patterns which are familiar to every student of urban life. Sociologists have sometimes claimed the ability to tell by a man's address within the city what his religion, his politics, his social class, and his general outlook and philosophy of life are likely to be. However exaggerated this claim may be in specific detail, ordinary observation in the larger American cities confirms the main outlines of this proposition. We find in almost every such metropolis a Gold Coast, a Bohemian quarter, a rooming-house area, slums, exclusive suburbs for the *nouveaux riche,* as well as one or more immigrant ghettos, each with its distinctive institutions and modes of life and its own patterns of thought.

Honolulu is neither old enough nor large enough to have evolved such clearly defined and extensive cultural islands as New York, Chicago, or Los Angeles, but it does have or once had its distinctive Chinatown, Hell's Half Acre, Portuguese Punchbowl, Tourist Waikiki, "Silk-Stocking" Manoa, and numerous immigrant "camps." Much of the social history of Hawaii could be written around the peculiarities of life within these cultural communities and the struggles between them.[9] It is possible here, however, only to suggest a few basic propositions regarding the way in which the racial or ethnic ghettos have functioned within the larger community of Honolulu.

Probably the first impressive fact about the ethnic communities in Honolulu, as compared with those of most cities in continental United States, is the relative absence of sharply marked boundaries between them. Like every other city to which peoples of alien cultures have been attracted, Honolulu has provided the immigrants with a place, however humble and inadequate, in which to live and to transplant the essential institutions of the homeland, but these voluntary ghettos are without walls and they commonly blend with their environment. The observer finds it difficult to discover where one racial community leaves off and its neighbor begins; thus it is that the geographic areas used in the enumeration of the census are rarely small enough or so peculiarly laid out as to enclose only the members of a single ethnic group. Neither Honolulu nor any one of the other towns and cities of Hawaii has now or ever has had solid racial tracts comparable to the Black Belts, the Little Tokyos, or the Little Sicilys so common in Mainland cities.

The foreign settlement in Honolulu in 1853 was too small (1,180 persons) and too cosmopolitan to develop any differential racial com-

---

[9]The distinctive life within the racial camps on the plantations and in the numerous non-plantation rural areas is an equally fascinating story, which has as yet been only partially told.

munities, and it was not until 1866 that the census even recorded population data by "subdistricts." The fifteen areas into which the Honolulu district was then divided, extending from Maunalua at the southeast extremity to Moanalua at the other, had varying proportions of the four ethnic groups specified in that census—Natives, Half-castes, Chinese, and Other Foreigners. The foreigners had only slightly penetrated the outlying areas at either end of the Honolulu district, but they were well represented in all seven of the more centrally situated subdistricts. Only the Chinese manifested any marked tendency to concentrate residentially, with somewhat more than half of their entire Honolulu population of 370 confined in the area adjacent to the harbor, which subsequently came to be known as Chinatown, but even here the Chinese constituted less than 6 per cent of the total.

With the city's growth in population, the possibilities of building separate communities for the different ethnic groups naturally also increased. By 1884 for example, the Chinese population of Honolulu had increased to more than five thousand persons, of whom 73 per cent resided within the Chinatown district. This, incidentally, was the period when anti-Chinese agitation was at its height and the concentration of these immigrants, together with their characteristic institutions, provided critics with tangible evidence that "they could never be assimilated." One such observer in 1882 comments as follows:

If you will ride slowly through the Chinese quarter, with your eyes open, you will go to your home with food for much thought. You find watchmakers' and jewelers' shops, tinshops, shoe-shops, tailor shops, saddle and harness-shops, furniture-shops, cabinet shops and bakeries, all run by Chinamen with Chinese workmen. While in the Chinese stores, which crowd each other in the Chinese quarter, and dot every street throughout the city and country you can find anything you want.[10]

Within another twenty years, Chinatown was definitely on the decline, although somewhat more than 40 per cent of the 9,000 Chinese of Honolulu in 1900 still lived in a small area of about a third of a square mile including and surrounding the original settlement. In 1960 there were still the vestiges of the old Chinatown as reflected in the scattered shops along Pauahi, Maunakea, and Smith Streets [11] and the Taoist Temples and Society Halls found over a somewhat wider area. The population of Chinese ancestry resident within the

[10] "The Chinese in Hawaii," *The Friend*, XXXI, No. 11 (1882), 114.
[11] The Chinese population of this very restricted area of only twenty-five acres had declined from 1,358 in 1920 to 851 in 1930 and in 1960 numbered less than three hundred.

same small area had in the meantime declined to 1,596 persons, which was roughly 5 per cent of the total Chinese population in the city and only 15.2 per cent of the total population of the area.

Portuguese, Japanese, Korean, Puerto Rican, and Filipino communities in Honolulu have experienced much the same cycle of growth and decline, following closely the order in which they have arrived in the city. The peak of Portuguese concentration, chiefly on the slopes of Punchbowl Crater and in the upper portions of Kalihi Valley, appears to have been reached by 1920, when settlements of 2,805 and 793 persons of Portuguese ancestry were reported in these two small areas respectively. Ten years later the Portuguese enumerated in approximately the same areas were notably lower (2,086) in the Punchbowl area and somewhat higher in the upper Kalihi area but still significantly large in both. Distinctive Catholic churches in each of these areas serve as integrating centers for what still remains of the once dominant Portuguese communities.

The Japanese, with their very much larger population in Honolulu since 1920, have been able to maintain their separate communities with greater effectiveness than any of the other ethnic groups. There were already in 1900, when the Japanese constituted only 15.7 per cent of the total population in Honolulu, clearly defined camps or communities consisting exclusively of members of that ethnic group, but the enumeration districts were too large to reflect the facts adequately. In 1920, however, when the 24,000 Japanese in Honolulu made up nearly 30 per cent of the city's total, there were numerous points of heavy concentration where the traditional institutions and patterns of homeland life could be partially duplicated. Especially significant were the settlements of Japanese fishermen in the Palama, River Street, and Kakaako areas adjacent to the harbor, and of truck gardeners, fruit and flower growers, and poultry and hog raisers in some of the outlying areas such as Kalihi, the Sheridan and McCully tracts, Moiliili, and Waialae regions.

In the 1930's there were still some twenty-five Japanese "camps" scattered over the city, within which the population was almost exclusively of Japanese ancestry. Here the characteristic institutions of the bath, Buddhist temples, Shinto shrines, language schools, *sumo* grounds, and teahouses helped to preserve an essentially Japanese climate and atmosphere, especially for the immigrant generation during the period of their adjustment to life in the city. It is still fairly easy to recognize the major centers of Japanese, but a number of the older communities in the central and transitional areas—the River

Street-Aala Park and the Kakaako sections—have virtually disappeared in the face of urban renewal and the pressure of business and industry. The points of heaviest concentration of Japanese populations and institutions in 1960 were in the Moiliili-McCully and the Palolo areas, three census tracts in which they represented from 63 to 69 per cent of the total population, although all the Japanese of these three tracts represented only 13 per cent of the entire Japanese population in Honolulu.

Even the smaller ethnic groups in Honolulu, including the Filipinos, Koreans, Puerto Ricans, and even the Negroes, have shown the same tendency to seek each other out for comfort and mutual support during the early periods of adjustment to the city. As the last of the immigrant groups to settle in Honolulu, the Filipinos have had relatively little choice as to residential quarters. During the first three decades of sizeable settlement in Honolulu, they were most heavily concentrated in a portion of the slum centering around the intersection of Liliha and King Streets, and in 1950 more than half of the total Filipino population of Honolulu were housed within a radius of less than a half mile of that intersection. Even in 1960 the two census tracts on either side of Liliha Street still had the highest ratios of Filipino residents—24.4 and 29.5 per cent—although the outward thrust of the city and urban renewal, as well as the rising affluence among the Filipinos themselves, had resulted in an expansion into the working class areas of Palama and Kalihi. Of the seven ethnic groups for whom the distribution by census tracts was available in 1960, the Filipinos were most highly concentrated within a limited area, with 57.5 per cent of their total Honolulu population resident in only 12 of the 72 census tracts of the city, all in the Liliha-Palama and Kalihi areas.

By way of contrast with the Filipinos, the Hawaiians and Part-Hawaiians stand out as ethnic groups with relatively little tendency toward residential segregation. Except for the census tracts in which the Papakolea Hawaiian Homes and certain public housing projects are located, the two Hawaiian groups are widely distributed over the city, with, however, some over-representation in the lower income areas. It appears paradoxical to most observers that the Hawaiians, with the least native disposition toward residential or other ethnic exclusiveness, should provide the only instances of complete racial segregation in the Hawaiian Homes Commission tracts such as Papakolea, Waimanalo, and Waianae, where by act of Congress only persons with 50 per cent or more Hawaiian blood may obtain leaseholds.

The Koreans, being one of the smaller of the immigrant groups, have never succeeded in establishing a separate community of their own in Honolulu or a single integrated center for their cultural life, although small settlements have existed since 1930 in the Palama district and on the slopes of Punchbowl among the Portuguese. The Puerto Ricans, whose number in Honolulu has been consistently less than the Koreans, have been much more sharply segregated in two restricted settlements, one in the Palama district and the other in upper Kalihi Valley, where somewhat more than one-fourth of their entire Honolulu population were still resident in 1950. The Negroes of Honolulu have commonly been identified in the popular mind with the slum area of Smith Street, and it is widely assumed that this last ethnic group to emerge in Hawaii is largely confined to this one disorganized area of Honolulu. Actually only a very small number— 31 persons or less than 3 per cent of the entire Negro population of the city—were living in the Smith Street area in 1960. Like the Koreans, they have always been rather widely dispersed over the city.

With the exception of the Haoles, all of the immigrant groups in Hawaii have made their initial adjustment to the city environment in the poorer economic areas—the slum sections surrounding the central business district of the city where residential rents are the cheapest or in sections not yet devoted to residential purposes. The level of housing especially, but the plane of living generally, has been low in these immigrant ghettos, whether situated within the central slum areas [12] or in the agricultural camps farther out from the center.

As the immigrants have improved their economic status, and as their children have put pressure upon them to live according to American standards, they have tended to leave the ghetto and to settle in better residential areas, either with other members of their own ethnic group or more commonly in a cosmopolitan section. An interesting example of the former is the Bingham Tract, sometimes known as "Chinese Hollywood," where in the middle 1920's a considerable number of families of Chinese ancestry sought to establish homes on an American pattern to take the place of their former abodes in Chinatown. One of the significant developments was the invasion of this area by non-Chinese, as the more prosperous Chinese pushed on to other districts with still higher prestige. At the present time, the population of Bingham Tract is thoroughly cosmopolitan

[12]"The Ghetto and the Slum," *Social Process*, IX, No. 2 (December, 1930), 206-215.

in character, although the Chinese still constitute somewhat more than their normal proportion of the whole.

The tendency to seek out as neighbors others with similar tastes and values has been no less evident among the Haoles than the other immigrant groups. The one distinguishing trait of the European and American settlements in Honolulu is their location in the better residential areas of the city. As revealed already in the census of 1884, when somewhat more than a quarter of all the European and American residents of Honolulu had settled in the cooler sections of Nuuanu Valley, the Haoles have always been found disproportionately in the high prestige areas—on the heights, in the valleys, and along the seashore. In the two censuses of 1920 and 1930, for which detailed data are available, the Other Caucasians were heavily concentrated in eight major areas—upper Nuuanu Valley, Manoa Valley, Waikiki, Kahala, Alewa Heights, Pacific Heights, Makiki Heights, and Maunalani. World War II brought about numerous changes in these upper class settlements through the evacuation to continental United States of some of their residents and the consequent invasion of these areas by members of other ethnic groups, as well as the rise of newer areas of residential exclusiveness, such as Wailupe Peninsula, Portlock Road, and Kailua.

The portions of the city devoted to military housing and to tourist hotels and apartments have reported a disproportionately high ratio of Caucasians, according to the censuses of both 1950 and 1960. In 1950, Waikiki's proportion of Caucasians (67.2 per cent) was almost three times their percentage in the city as a whole, and ten years later the Caucasian ratio (60 per cent) in that tourist center was still well over twice what would be expected on the basis of the entire city. Similarly, some of the census tracts in close proximity to military bases reported ratios of Caucasians in 1960 as high as 99.6 per cent, thus lending support to the erroneous impression that the residents of Honolulu, or at least the Caucasians, were increasingly disposed toward residential segregation on the basis of race.

The tendency to form separate communities, which is characteristic of all newly arrived immigrant groups in large metropolitan centers, manifests one important variation among the various racial groups in Honolulu. This is a pronounced tendency for the several racial islands to become rather quickly fused with each other. Not only are the physical barriers between the several racial communities less distinct than in most Mainland communities, but the meager barriers which do exist tend to disappear more rapidly here. What was once Chinatown, Little Portugal, or a Japanese camp loses its Chinese, Portuguese, or Japanese atmosphere and becomes increasingly cosmopolitan in appearance and outlook as persons of other ethnic groups move into the area.

The experience of Honolulu's Chinatown is fairly typical of what has happened to most racial colonies in the city. By way of introducing a detailed discussion of this problem, Glick characterizes the situation in the middle 1930's as follows.

The American who sails to Hawaii from San Francisco, site of the largest and most famous Chinatown in the United States, looks for a similar community in Honolulu, especially after he learns that there are 3,000 more people of Chinese ancestry in Honolulu than in San Francisco. But he is surprised to see that the so-called "Chinatown" is not an exclusively Chinese quarter, but a district in which among the Chinese are interspersed numerous Japanese firms, with here and there a business operated by Koreans, Filipinos and white-Americans (haoles). On the streets he may see not only Cantonese faces, but faces of every racial group living in the Islands. From the second-story windows and balconies look down representatives of all the groups which make up Honolulu's polyglot community.[13]

He points out further that even in the eighties when the Chinese were most severely criticized for their clannishness and unassimilability, Chinatown was never composed exclusively of Chinese, and writers of the period referred to the "large number of natives who lived in the Chinese quarter." The two major Chinatown fires left "many Hawaiians and some 'half-castes'" homeless in 1886 and large numbers of Japanese and some Portuguese were similarly affected in 1900. By 1920 the old Chinatown provided homes for almost as many Japanese as Chinese, in addition to sizeable groups of Hawaiians, Part-Hawaiians, Filipinos, Portuguese, and Other Caucasians. By 1940 the Japanese in the district were in excess of the Chinese, and by 1960, the central Chinatown area was less than a quarter Chinese, while over a third of the population were Filipinos.

The corresponding dispersion of each of the ethnic groups, as the need for the racial ghetto declines, is equally evident. The Hawaiians and Part-Hawaiians have always been the most widely and evenly distributed of all the ethnic groups in Honolulu. Of the immigrant groups, one would expect that those with the longest experience in the city and the smallest total numbers would be least residentially segregated, and this is roughly the case. A study of the distribution of ethnic

[13]Clarence Glick, "Residential Dispersion of Urban Chinese," *Social Process in Hawaii*, II (1936), 28-34.

groups by census tracts in 1940 and 1950 reveals that the "Hawaiians, Chinese, and Others (Korean, Puerto Ricans, and Negroes) tended to be relatively least segregated and moving in the direction of less segregation in 1950. The Caucasian and Filipino groups tended to be relatively most segregated and moving in the direction of greater segregation between 1940 and 1950." [14] With only one exception of a district within a naval reservation, all five of the major ethnic groups in 1960 were represented in all seventy-two of the census tracts of Honolulu. Even the smallest and the most recent group to appear, the 1,319 Negroes enumerated in 1960, had one or more residents in all but ten of the seventy-two tracts, and the second smallest group of 3,828 full Hawaiians was represented in all seventy-one of the civilian census tracts.

A minor deviation from the general tendency of all ethnic groups to be gradually absorbed within the interracial melange which characterizes Honolulu as a whole has been the temporary appearance of small concentrations of a given racial group from time to time in a new residential development. The emergence shortly after the war of a cluster of homes on the slopes of Tantalus, belonging to upper income families of Chinese ancestry and facetiously referred to as Mandarin Heights, is a case in point. At the time this tract of land was opened to competitive bidding, the people most favorably situated with ready and adequate cash and at the same time most desirous of investing some of it in preferred residential lots happened to be Chinese, but with the passage of time, the predominantly Chinese character of the area is gradually being lost. Similar concentrations of Haoles have occurred in the vicinity of Koko Head and on windward Oahu and of middle class Okinawans close to Wahiawa. All such groupings, however, whether based upon economic class, racial preference, friendship, or a combination of similar factors, can persist only for a limited period of time under the dynamic conditions which prevail in modern Hawaii. The long-term trend is clearly in the direction of a residential diffusion of ethnic stocks and the creation of a community where people no longer take account to any serious degree of the racial ancestry of their neighbors.

[14]Douglas S. Yamamura and Raymond Sakumoto, "Residential Segregation in Honolulu," *Social Process in Hawaii*, XVIII (1954), 45. The authors explain that the recent arrival in Honolulu of plantation laborers from the 1946 importation is partly responsible for the temporary reversal of the trend among the Filipinos. The increased provision of housing for defense workers and for the dependents of service personnel affords a partial explanation of the increased segregation among the Caucasians.

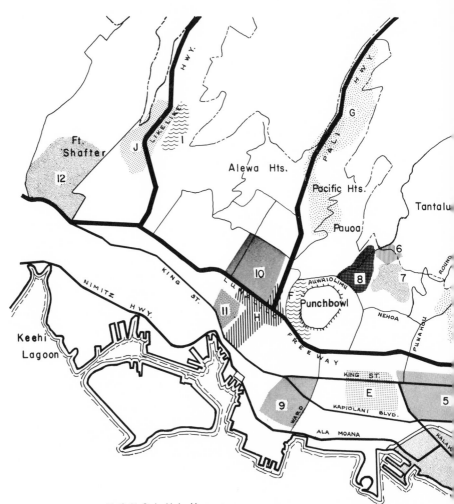

H O N O L U L U

PAST (1930)		PRESENT (1960)	
A	Waialae Farming Area	1	Wailupe
B	Woodlawn	2	Kahala
C	Manoa Farming Area	3	Palolo
D	Manoa	4	Waikiki
E	Sheridan Tract	5	Moiliili—McCully
F	Portuguese Punchbowl	6	Mandarin Heights
G	Nuuanu—Pacific Heights	7	Haole Makiki
H	Old Chinatown	8	Papakolea
I	Kalihi-Uka	9	Kakaako
J	Kalihi-Uka Farming Area	10	Kuakini
		11	Hell's Half Acre
		12	Fort Shafter

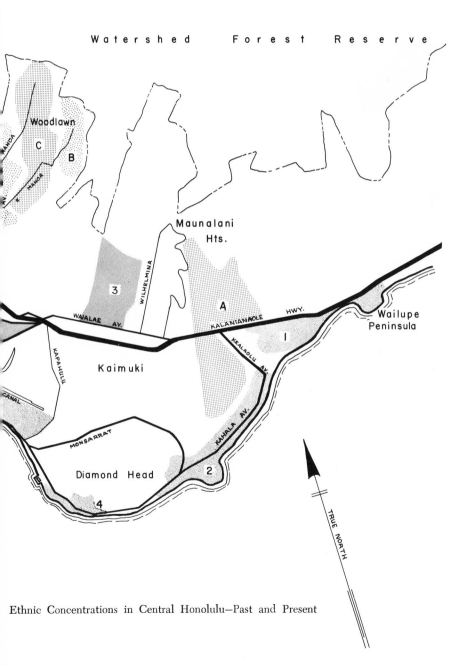

Ethnic Concentrations in Central Honolulu—Past and Present

4

HOW DO THEY LIVE?

Few, if any, areas on earth outside of Hawaii have experienced such revolutionary economic transformations within so brief a span of time. Within a period of less than two centuries, the basic mode of supporting human life has evolved from a stone-age subsistence economy to a state of advanced capitalism which is paralleled in few other parts of the world. At the time of Captain Cook's discovery of Hawaii, the Islanders derived their livelihood directly from the cultivation of the soil and the sea within the immediate vicinity of their abodes, and the exchange of either goods or services was virtually absent. Cut off from their nearest continental or island neighbors by many hundreds of miles of open water, the Hawaiians had to rely exclusively upon the meager range of plant and animal life within the Islands. There were no mineral resources available within the archipelago for the making of metal tools, and the natives were thus forced to rely upon the stone or shell tools which they could fashion out of the materials at hand.[1]

The explorers and traders, who began to visit Hawaii after word of Captain Cook's discovery was publicized in Europe and America, initiated the Islanders into the ways of Western trade and thus indirectly removed the foundations of the native economy centered upon the production and consumption of the two Island staples of fish and poi. Part of this story is told in the declining numbers of native population living on the land and their attraction to the towns and urban centers, as indicated in the preceding chapter. It is more graphically

[1] Andrew W. Lind, "Interracial Marraiage as Affecting Divorce in Hawaii," *Sociogy* pp. 24-38.

told, however, not in the census statistics, which in any case are very meager during this early period, but in the descriptive accounts by traders, missionaries, and other visitors. From such sources it is possible to get a sense of the high status value which the natives attached to Western clothing, diet, housing, religion, and learning, and of the corresponding decline in prestige of things Hawaiian.

Unfortunately, the early censuses of Hawaii tell little about the transformations in the modes of securing a livelihood brought on by the introduction of trade during the first half of the nineteenth century. The census of 1853, for example, includes no reference whatsoever to occupation, and it was not until 1866 that any specific account was taken in the censuses of the economic aspects of Island life. The presence, however, of 2,119 non-Polynesians in 1853, of whom all but 367 had resided in the Islands for at least a year, suggests the growing influence of trade. It may be assumed that the great majority of the foreigners followed a way of life which required the importation of foreign commodities and some means of support other than simple subsistence farming. In addition, the concentration within the district of Honolulu of more than ten thousand natives—one-seventh of the entire population of the Polynesian race—points strongly to the important role which trade had assumed in the life of the region.

A special tabulation of the population of Honolulu in 1847 reveals a community almost wholly organized around the principles of trade and the exchange of services. The list of 441 persons with occupations in the rising town reflects a wide range of services, including those of blacksmith, boat builder, carpenter, mason, painter, tailor, shoemaker, bookbinder, baker, engraver, clerk, pilot, auctioneer, consul, lawyer, surveyor, barber, and sexton, to mention only a few.[2] Their services were divided between the personnel of the large number of trading and whaling vessels which visited the Islands and the residents of the region, including many of the native Hawaiians residing in the rural areas. An increasing number of the Islanders were living on the margins of the two competing economies, deriving most of their livelihood from the cultivation of their own *kuleanas* but also earning some money for the purchase of trade goods from the sale of farm surplus or from an occasional day of work with the government.

As the trading economy became more pervasive throughout the Islands during the second half of the century, there was an increasing

[2]In the admittedly incomplete listing of occupations among natives, all 115 were in skilled trades, including 60 blacksmiths, 12 carpenters, 4 masons, 19 tailors, 9 shoemakers, 6 bookbinders, 4 printers, and 1 engraver. *Ibid.*, p. 321.

interest in securing through the census an accurate count of the persons employed in each major occupation. The census of 1866 for the first time reported the figures for the entire population engaged under five major occupational categories, designated and defined as follows: 7,154 freeholders, presumably natives continuing to live on their own *kuleanas;* 8,258 agriculturists, "those known to have some considerable amount of land devoted to agricultural and grazing purposes"; 1,146 mechanics, "those generally understood as such, native and foreign included"; 5,025 laborers, "those who were permanently employed, generally on contract," and probably including most of the unskilled workers on the plantations; and 512 "professionalists, those of the learned professions, as generally understood by that term." [3] Although one cannot determine how complete the reporting under these vaguely defined categories actually was or, indeed, whether the terms were mutually exclusive, it provides some rough indication of how Hawaii's people secured their livelihood and, when taken together with other data in the census, suggests that well over half of the natives were still living under a predominantly subsistence economy.

Thirty years later, in 1896, the sugar plantations had emerged as the major factor in the Hawaiian economy, and although it was still impossible to define precisely the total effect of Western influences, the plantations had obviously assumed a dominant position. Assuming the accuracy of the census returns on occupation, it appears likely that well over 90 per cent of the gainfully employed were engaged in occupations associated with the plantations or in other fields associated with commerce and trade. Owing to the very large immigration of adult workers for the plantations during the previous thirty years, the proportion of employed persons to the total population had reached the amazingly high figure of 50.8 per cent. As a consequence also of the central position of plantation agriculture in the economic life of the region, nearly two-thirds (61.9 per cent) of all employed persons were unskilled laborers, performing the menial and arduous tasks of hoeing, cutting, and carrying which the early plantation regime required. As nearly as can be ascertained from the census, 78.2 per cent of all employed persons were engaged in agriculture or fishing, with the remaining 21.8 per cent performing all the services of trade and commerce, domestic and professional services, and mechanical skills.

During the following period of thirty-five or forty years, the plantation experienced its maximum development in economic influence and efficiency. Sugar and pineapple production not only supplied the major

[3]Census of the Kona District, Island of Oahu, taken December 7, 1866.

source of livelihood for Hawaii's population; their influence also extended to almost the whole of the economic structure of the Islands. Such apparently unrelated economic enterprises as transportation, banking, public utilities, merchandising, and the operation of hotels were financed and operated by the promoters of the sugar and pineapple plantations. The concentration of economic control through the agency system of the "Big Five" also made possible economies in operation which could not otherwise be attained, and Hawaii acquired a reputation for scientific production of plantation crops which is unparalleled in any part of the world. The available land for agricultural use was seriously limited in Hawaii, and any further expansion of the industry depended, therefore, upon increased production per unit of land. The table tells this story with respect to the sugar industry in abbreviated and dramatic form.[4]

5. SUGAR ACREAGE AND YIELDS, 1895-1965

	ACRES HARVESTED	TONS OF SUGAR	TONS PER ACRE
1895	47,339	153,419	3.2
1900	66,773	289,544	4.3
1920	114,100	556,871	4.8
1930	136,136	930,627	6.8
1940	136,417	976,677	7.2
1950	109,405	960,961	8.9
1960	103,584	935,744	9.0
1965	109,600	1,217,667	11.1

Despite the widespread belief that the peak of sugar production had been reached in the early nineties of the last century, the area devoted to sugar cultivation continued to expand until the middle thirties, and during the succeeding twenty years there has been a slow increase in production although the acreage has significantly declined. Most striking, of course, is the slow but steady increase in the yields per acre, which by the middle sixties were more than three times what they were seventy years earlier and unrivaled in any sugar-producing area of the world.

Even more impressive as affecting the occupational outlets for the people of Hawaii is the story of steadily increasing sugar production along with a rapid decline in the number of workers.

[4]Except for the very much shorter time span involved, much the same story could be told with respect to the pineapple industry.

6. *PLANTATION EMPLOYEES AND SUGAR PRODUCTION, 1882-1962*

	Employees	Tons of Sugar	Tons per Employee
1882	10,243	57,088	5.6
1892	20,536	131,308	6.4
1912	47,345	595,258	12.6
1932	51,427	1,024,354	19.9
1942	26,371	870,109	33.0
1952	18,193	1,020,450	56.1
1962	10,960	1,120,011	102.2

Needless to say, the production of 102 tons of sugar for every employee on the Hawaiian plantations in 1962 as compared with 5.6 tons for every employee just eighty years earlier is primarily a reflection of the amazing technological advancements within the sugar industry itself. Thus, although the number of employees remained fairly constant for more than thirty years and then dropped to about a fifth of its peak figure, sugar production continued to mount. The striking decline in the number of workers in the sugar industry after 1932 is, of course, an adjustment of management to the increasing costs of labor occasioned by the extension of federal labor legislation to Hawaii, unionization, and the growing demand for labor in other fields.

The most recent phase in the evolution of Hawaii's economy, marked by the declining dominance of sugar and pineapple production and the rise in commercial, tourist, and defense industries, is largely confined to the period since 1930, but the transition to the new order was evident considerably earlier. Although the absolute number of persons employed in agriculture remained relatively constant from 1900 to 1930, the proportion of all persons gainfully employed in agriculture declined steadily. Prior to 1930, there was a striking contrast in the distribution by industry of the employed population of Hawaii as compared with that of continental United States, with roughly twice as high a proportion engaged in agriculture and only half the proportion in manufacturing, transportation, and trade in the Islands as on the Mainland.

The increase in occupational outlets in Hawaii during the first three decades of the present century occurred chiefly in the fields related to trade, including manufacturing, transportation, and clerical pursuits. The number of persons engaged in these four related areas of employment was trebled, while their proportion of the total number of gainfully employed increased from 17.9 per cent in 1900 to 31.9 per cent

7. *GAINFULLY EMPLOYED, 1872-1930**

	Number					Per Cent				
	1872	1900	1910	1920	1930	1872	1900	1910	1920	1930
Agriculture	21,022	56,056	56,239	56,244	61,811	86.0	62.2	55.7	50.3	40.1
Manufacturing, Mechanical Industries	2,115	9,310	15,345	18,194	23,018	8.7	10.3	15.2	16.3	14.9
Transportation, Communication		3,785	6,723	7,781	9,602		4.2	6.6	7.0	6.2
Trade	728	3,065	5,831	7,343	10,572	3.0	3.4	5.8	6.6	6.9
Public Service			2,842	6,282	20,052			2.8	5.6	13.0
Professional Service	582	1,742	2,601	4,117	8,230	2.3	1.9	2.6	3.7	5.3
Domestic and Personal Service		16,214	9,434	8,466	13,070		18.0	9.3	7.6	8.5
Clerical Occupations			1,807	3,286	5,954			1.8	2.9	3.9
All Other			372	169	1,953			.2		1.2
TOTAL	24,447	90,172	101,194	111,882	154,262	100.0	100.0	100.0	100.0	100.0

*A serious limitation in the use of census data to measure occupational trends results from the inconsistencies from one census period to the next in the classification of the various occupations. It is especially unfortunate for present purposes that the U. S. Bureau of the Census found it necessary prior to the 1940 enumeration to change radically the industrial and occupational categories utilized, making comparisons between the data of 1930 and 1940 difficult. Illustrative of the lack of consistency in census classifications is the striking shift in the number of persons classified as domestic and personal service workers between 1900 and 1930. In most of the other major categories, there is evidence of a considerable degree of consistency between the various census periods.

in 1930. Although no very large number of persons was involved in professional services as compared to the total, the more than four-fold increase between 1900 and 1930 points to a notable improvement in the plane of living during that period. The more striking increase, both in absolute numbers and rate, from 2,842 in 1910 to 20,052 in 1930, occurred in the area called public service and was a reflection chiefly of Hawaii's mounting importance as America's military outpost in the Pacific. Persons classified as "soldiers, sailors, and marines" increased from 1,608 in 1910 to 4,366 in 1920, and to 16,291 in 1930. According to the 1940 census, shortly before the outbreak of World War II in the Pacific, the military personnel in Hawaii, excluding commissioned officers, professional and clerical workers, and craftsmen, had increased to 26,233.

The data in Table 8, while not strictly comparable with those of the earlier periods chiefly because of the markedly different era in Hawaii's economic history to which they relate, further confirm some of the trends already outlined. The decline in the proportion of all workers engaged in agriculture, so apparent in the period prior to 1930 when the plantations were in their prime, took the form after 1930 of a decided drop in the numbers as well. From a peak of nearly 62,000 agricultural workers in 1930, the numbers so engaged dropped to somewhat less than 16,000 during the next thirty years, and although a decline in both the number and the proportion of workers engaged in agriculture has long been noted in continental United States and elsewhere, it has rarely occurred with such rapidity as in Hawaii.

During the first half of the 1940's, Hawaii experienced a wartime boom in which workers of every type were at a premium, many Islanders acquired fortunes, and the loss of employment opportunities in agriculture was greatly exceeded by new developments in other areas, most notably in public administration.[5] By 1950, however, the artificial wartime prosperity had begun to fade, and it appeared that the increase of 7.8 per cent in the total number of employment outlets between 1940 and 1950 was not keeping pace with the 10 per cent increase in the labor force during the same decade, as reflected in the 8.4 per cent unemployment rate.

One additional economic shift during the forties with far reaching consequences on race relations following the war was the sudden transformation of Hawaii from a region of minimal labor organization

[5]The mounting number of persons engaged in military duties in Hawaii, which increased from about 29,000 reported in "national defense industries" in 1940 to 52,881 in 1960, is, of course, not reflected directly in Table 8, relating only to employed civilian workers.

8. EMPLOYED CIVILIAN WORKERS, 1940, 1950, 1960

	Number			Per Cent of Total			Per Cent Mainland
	1940	1950	1960	1940	1950	1960	1960
Agriculture, Forestry, Fisheries	54,629	31,806	15,982	35.5	19.0	7.6	6.7
Construction	10,817	11,653	19,882	7.0	7.0	9.5	5.9
Manufacturing	15,454	21,474	33,622	10.0	12.8	16.1	27.9
Transportation, Communications, Public Utilities	8,515	13,450	16,734	5.6	8.0	8.1	6.9
Trade, Finance, Business	26,944	38,978	51,584	17.5	23.3	24.5	24.9
Personal Service	15,067	10,812	14,285	9.8	6.5	6.8	6.0
Entertainment and Recreation Service	1,487	2,442	2,394	1.0	1.5	1.1	.8
Professional and Related Services	11,647	17,321	26,356	7.6	10.2	12.6	11.7
Public Administration	7,569	18,436	22,464	4.9	11.0	10.7	5.0
Not Reported and Other	1,544	1,199	6,190	1.0	.7	3.0	4.1
TOTAL	153,796	167,571	209,370	100.0	100.0	100.0	100.0

to one of the most highly organized areas in the United States. The plantation, by virtue of its concern for the conservation and control of its laborers, especially during the early years when the supply was limited, necessarily resisted vigorously any attempts to organize its workers. As recently as 1939, it could be authoritatively stated that:

In comparison with the highly integrated character of industrial management, the organization of labor in the Territory is meager. . . . the plantation system continues to be paternalistic. Employee organizations do exist on the plantations, but they take the form of recreational and social clubs, or of religious groups, usually along racial lines. . . . Estimates of total membership by union officials vary from 3,500 to 6,000 members. Even if the larger figure is accepted as accurate, it would indicate that less than one twenty-fifth of the gainfully employed are unionized.[6]

The severe limitations imposed upon plantation laborers during the war, when they were frozen to their jobs at wages considerably lower than those of defense workers on Oahu, prepared the field for wholesale unionization when the war was over. Thus the U.S. Department of Labor Report in 1947 summarized the transformation as follows:

Until 1944 Hawaii was one of the least organized areas in the United States, but within two years it had become one of the most highly organized areas.[7]

Another war, in Korea commencing in 1950, followed by continued military activities around the Pacific basin and mounting travel within the Pacific, especially of tourists, brought about another expansion in Hawaii's labor market, as striking in its effects and longer lasting than that of World War II. The highest rate of growth in employment (70.6 per cent) occurred between 1950 and 1960 in the construction industries, although the numerical increase was heaviest in the fields of manufacturing and of trade, finance and business.

Hawaii's growing comparability with continental United States, as revealed in the last two columns of Table 8, was considerably greater in 1960 than it had been at any previous time. The most important differences appear in the lower proportions of Hawaii's workers engaged in manufacturing—a difference which Hawaii's limited natural resources and physical isolation seem destined to continue—and the higher proportions in construction and in public administration. Hawaii's decided over-proportion in the building and construction industries is a consequence of the shift in Island economy toward

[6]United States Department of Labor, *Labor in the Territory of Hawaii* (Washington: U.S. Printing Office, 1940), pp. 199, 202.
[7]James H. Shoemaker, *The Economy of Hawaii in 1947* (Washington: U.S. Printing Office, 1948), p. 188.

defense and tourism since the war and can scarcely be expected to
continue indefinitely in the future. Public administration, on the other
hand, is one field in which Hawaii's strategic position in both military
and civilian affairs seems likely to place heavy demands upon the
Islands for some time to come. If in 1960 the 52,881 persons in the
military services were included in the labor force, it would place well
over a quarter of the workers in public administration, as compared
with 8.0 per cent in the whole of the United States.

FINDING AN ECONOMIC PLACE

The initial steps in the economic adjustment of most of Hawaii's
immigrants were taken for them by the planters who brought them to
the Islands. The labor contracts or agreements, specifying wages,
remuneration, and length of service, were signed in the homeland, and
after the immigrants' arrival in Hawaii, conformity to the plantation
regime, rather than personal initiative, was the major requirement of
the workers. The control over labor, which was essential to the effectiveness of the plantation throughout the pioneering period of the
nineteenth and early twentieth centuries, extended far beyond the
considerations of hours, wages, and working conditions to matters of
housing, food, language, habits of sleep and recreation, and even religion and politics. Even though these controls, under the conditions
prevailing in Hawaii, were mild as compared with most plantation
frontiers, the workers were generally disposed to seek greener pas-
tures after the expiration of their initial contracts. As a result, until the
early thirties the planters were constantly compelled to renew their
labor force by additional importation.

The conditions of plantation labor, throughout most of this period,
seem onerous by present standards, but compared to conditions prevailing in their home communities, the inducements were adequate to
bring an almost unlimited supply of workers. The Chinese, for example, who were recruited in 1852 for a term of five years at a wage
of $36 per annum in addition to their passage, food, clothing, and
house, could readily have been obtained in sufficient numbers to
supply all the labor demands of the Hawaiian plantations. The planters
themselves in the early eighties helped to establish the barriers to
further Chinese immigration for fear that a racial monopoly of the
labor supply might be created and thus threaten control of the
industry. The following table measures roughly the flow of the different ethnic groups through the sugar plantations of the Territory and
reflects the operation of the processes just mentioned.

9. SUGAR PLANTATION EMPLOYEES BY RACE

	Number					Per Cent of Total					
	1882	1902	1922	1932	1942	1882	1902	1922	1932	1942	1952*
Hawaiian and Part-Hawaiian	2,575	1,493	966	615	816	25.1	3.5	4.4	1.2	2.4	
Portuguese	637	2,669	2,533	2,022	2,302	6.2	6.4	5.7	4.0	6.8	
Puerto Rican		2,036	1,715	797	646		4.8	3.9	1.6	1.9	
Other Caucasian	834		942	900	903	8.1		2.1	1.8	2.7	
Chinese	5,037	3,937	1,487	706	302	49.2	9.3	3.4	1.4	.9	
Japanese	15	31,029	16,992	9,395	10,397	.1	73.5	38.3	18.8	30.6	30.7
Korean			1,170	442				2.6	.9		
Filipino			18,189	34,915	18,135			41.0	69.9	53.4	51.7
All Others	1,145	1,078	408	155	445	11.2	2.5	.9	.3	1.3	
TOTAL	10,243	42,242	44,402	49,947	33,946						

*Figures for 1952, except for Japanese and Filipino, not available.

The complete dependence upon immigrant labor is evident from the beginning of plantation dominance in Hawaii, although the Hawaiians have continued to play a minor but important role as *lunas* (supervisors) and skilled workers down to the present day. The great bulk of the workers has been provided successively by three groups, with the Chinese dominant in the early eighties, the Japanese during the nineties and the first two decades of the present century, and the Filipinos in first position since that time. Especially evident is the rather rapid rate at which the Chinese and Koreans passed through the plantation stage of economic adjustment, in contrast to the Portuguese, whose number and proportion of the total remained relatively constant after the beginning of the century. The Portuguese, like the Hawaiians, were advanced to supervisory (*luna*) and skilled positions on the plantations more readily than the Oriental groups. The Other Caucasians (Haoles) have never constituted more than a token group among the plantation workers and have usually been confined to the skilled and supervisory levels.[8]

A major change in plantation labor since 1932 has been the increasing mechanization and the corresponding demand for skilled personnel to handle the machinery. In response to this development within the industry, as well as the declining occupational opportunities elsewhere following the depression and again after World War II, the children of the immigrant laborers have looked more favorably than formerly upon the plantation as an occupational outlet. The numerical and percentage increases of Japanese and Portuguese among plantation employees between 1932 and 1941 were almost wholly of the Island born and educated. Although the Filipinos, as the latest arrivals and the least fortunately situated of the ethnic groups, continue to provide most of the unskilled laborers on the plantations, they too have been able to improve their economic and social status by entering the skilled and supervisory levels.

Even unskilled plantation labor has acquired a far higher status following World War II. Partly as a consequence of federal and local legislation and the effective bargaining of a strong labor union, wages of the workers on the plantations have risen to a point such that the sugar industry has been able to boast that it "pays the highest, year-round agricultural wages in the world to its production workers," citing an average cash wage in 1964 of $17.60 daily plus added fringe

---

[8]Those listed as Other Caucasians in 1882 were the small number of Norwegian and German laborers who had recently arrived in the Islands. Numerous smaller groups, such as the South Sea Islanders, Negroes, and Mongolians, have classified as All Others.

10. GAINFULLY EMPLOYED MALES CLASSIFIED AS LABORERS, 1896-1960*

	NUMBER EMPLOYED					PER CENT OF TOTAL				
	1896	1910	1930	1950	1960†	1896	1910	1930	1950	1960†
Hawaiians	2,758	4,040	2,325	892		30.0	50.5	39.5	34.6	
Part-Hawaiians	348	569	959	2,062		25.5	24.9	22.1	20.0	
Portuguese	3,036 }	6,898 }	2,044 }	2,235	2,626	73.6 }	43.8 }	30.1 }	5.1	8.4
Other Caucasians	312 }		396 }			9.3 }		4.4 }		
Chinese	10,923	6,680	2,088	431	429	65.8	48.6	24.4	5.3	4.4
Japanese	14,394	33,871	12,754	7,482	5,183	87.5	76.8	35.9	16.3	9.9
Filipino			41,075	13,387	9,532			90.1	52.5	40.0
Korean			1,142	160				53.4	11.4	
Puerto Rican			1,455	851				78.2	34.4	
All Others	256	5,355	173	787		43.2	89.7	81.2	21.2	
TOTAL	32,027	57,413	64,411	27,277	21,293	61.9	65.0	53.6	22.5	15.6

*Some shift in the basis of classification of occupations between 1896 and 1910 and again between 1930 and 1950 may raise doubts as to the strict comparability of data. There is internal evidence, however, that the term "laborer" has carried a similar meaning throughout the period.

†Owing to the 1960 census practise of combining the Hawaiians and Koreans in the "All Others" category, the latter becomes meaningless and confusing for comparative purposes and is therefore omitted.

benefits of $6.50 to all adult, hourly rated employees, both field and factory.[9] Data available in the 1950 census, but not reported in such detail in the 1960 census, indicate that plantation labor no longer represented, as it once did, the bottom rung on the economic ladder in Hawaii—that median annual incomes of male laborers on "sugar farms" (plantations) were slightly higher than those of farmers and farm managers and substantially above those of nonagricultural laborers.

The changing record of persons listed in the census as laborers tells a somewhat similar story of the improving status of the various ethnic groups after some years of residence in the Islands. Within little more than half a century the Chinese have run the full cycle from an immigrant labor group to one in which unskilled labor is almost nonexistent. The Portuguese and Japanese, in that order, followed the Chinese in pushing out of the laboring class, and by 1930 the Portuguese had only 30.1 per cent of their employed males left in that class while the Japanese had a somewhat higher proportion. The slower rate of upward movement among the Filipinos is reflected in the fact that twenty-five years after most of them arrived in Hawaii more than half of their employed men were still classified as laborers and that in 1960 the proportion of Filipino men so designated was nearly three times that of all males in Hawaii. This is not a reflection upon the ability or ambition of the Filipinos so much as an indication of the handicaps which the latest arrivals in any immigrant situation are likely to encounter.

It is significant that of the two smaller immigrant groups which arrived at about the same time, the Puerto Ricans and the Koreans, the latter had by 1930 graduated out of the laboring class to a far greater degree than had the former, and insofar as comparable data are available at a later date, they indicate an increasing differential between the two groups.

The relative absence of Other Caucasians from the ranks of ordinary laborers, as revealed in the census data of 1896 and 1930, is, of course, consistent with the earlier stereotyped impressions of the Haoles as persons "of superior economic and social status." [10] If separate data for the Other Caucasians and the Portuguese were available for 1960, it would almost certainly reveal a proportion considerably less than 8.4 per cent for the former and a higher one for the latter. A relation-

[9]*Hawaii's Sugar News*, XV (March, 1965), 2.
[10]Romanzo Adams, *Interracial Marriage in Hawaii* (New York: The Macmillan Company, 1937), p. 115.

ship somewhat comparable to that between the Portuguese and the Haoles with respect to work as laborers is to be found between the Hawaiians and the Part-Hawaiians. Throughout the entire period since 1896 for which comparable data are available, the Part-Hawaiians were much less represented in the ranks of unskilled labor than the full Hawaiians, which parallels the experience of native and mixed-blood populations in other areas of the Pacific. It was not, however, until 1950 that the full Hawaiians were significantly over-represented in this area.

The parallel story of what happened to these groups as they moved out of ordinary labor pursuits is much more difficult to tell. There are many different paths to economic advancement and not all persons, even of the same group, have moved at the same rate of speed or followed the same route. Within the limits of this study it is possible to provide only one or two indices of the direction and the rate of the upward movement among the different ethnic groups.[11]

Among the most promising channels of advancement in status, if not always in economic position, are the professions, and the census record of participation in these occupations affords one of the most sensitive gauges of advancing prestige on the part of the several ethnic groups. Table 11 provides further evidence of the advantage which the Haole has enjoyed in Hawaii's occupational hierarchy, and which he still continues to enjoy, judging by the high rate of 17.9 per cent of the combined Caucasian men who were classified as professionals in 1960.[12] The advantage which the Hawaiians and especially the Part-Hawaiians enjoyed in the professions during the earlier census periods had largely disappeared before 1940. The Chinese, on the other hand, have greatly increased their representation in the professions from a low of 0.5 per cent in 1910 to 17.9 in 1960, second only to the Caucasians. The evidence presented earlier of the more rapid occupational advancement of the Koreans as compared with the Puerto Ricans is also confirmed in the table on the professions. The handicap encountered by the Filipinos in being last of the major groups to arrive on the scene continues to reflect itself in their very small proportion in the professions, but this strength is slowly increasing.

[11]More detailed accounts of developments among the various ethnic groups are available in the author's *An Island Community*, Chapter 11, and in "Mounting the Occupational Ladder in Hawaii," Romanzo Adams Social Research Laboratory Report 24 (January, 1957).

[12]An adequate index of the relative position of each ethnic group can be obtained by dividing its ratio in the professions by the ratio of the total working force in the professions. Thus, the 17.9 percentage of Caucasians in the professions in 1960 indicates that they had roughly 1.8 times their expected proportion in this field. The Chinese had 1.6 times their expected representation and the Japanese had approximately what would be expected.

11. GAINFULLY EMPLOYED MALES CLASSIFIED AS PROFESSIONAL, 1896-1960*

	Number Employed					Per Cent of Total				
	1896	1910	1930	1950	1960	1896	1910	1930	1950	1960
Hawaiian	132	126	242	93	†	1.4	1.6	4.1	3.6	†
Part-Hawaiian	54	71	293	649	†	4.0	3.1	6.7	6.3	†
Portuguese	30 }	444	180 }	4,232	5,589	.7 }	3.1	2.6 }	16.9	17.9
Other Caucasian	164 }		1,563 }			4.9 }		17.2 }		
Chinese	300	65	259	876	1,633	1.8	.5	3.0	10.7	16.6
Japanese	88	221	1,204	2,506	5,286	.5	.5	3.4	5.5	10.1
Filipino			268	296	424			.6	1.2	1.8
Korean			58	121	†			2.7	8.6	†
Puerto Rican			20	15	†			1.1	.9	†
All Others	13	23	32	138	†	2.2	.4	4.2	3.7	†
TOTAL	781	950	4,119	8,829	14,025	1.5	1.1	3.4	7.3	10.2

*There is somewhat greater reason to doubt the strict comparability of data between various census dates in this table than in Table 10.
†Not separately available.

Commerce and trade have afforded in Hawaii, as in other areas of immigrant settlement, effective media for the economic advancement of the new arrivals. The widely observed penchant of the Chinese for establishing themselves in business, if only as peddlers with their wealth in packs on their backs, found expression in Hawaii almost before the first immigrants had completed the terms of their contracts for plantation work, and as early as 1854 the planters were complaining that the Chinese were ambitious "to live without work—by store keeping, perhaps." Within less than ten years of the arrival of the bulk of the first large immigration of Chinese laborers, 60 per cent of the wholesale and retail merchandising establishments of the Territory were operated by Chinese. The advantage enjoyed by the Chinese in this area was naturally not as fully shared by the later immigrant groups, but the pattern established by them was followed to a considerable degree by the Japanese and Koreans.

The Filipinos, on the other hand, have found the field already well occupied, and it is possible also that there is less of a trading tradition among the Filipinos than among the other immigrant groups from the Orient. By 1950 the Chinese had 1.6 times their normal proportion of managers, officials, and proprietors, the Japanese had 1.2 times their expected proportion, while the Filipinos had less than a fourth of theirs. Similarly in the field of clerical and sales workers, the Chinese were greatly over-represented, the Japanese somewhat less so, and the Filipinos grossly under-represented.[13] It is especially noteworthy, in this connection, that by 1960 the disproportionate representation of the Chinese, Japanese, and Caucasians in these preferred occupations had been significantly reduced. The rise in occupational status of the Filipinos during this decade appears to have been chiefly as craftsmen and operatives.

There are important elements in their culture which have militated against success in business on the part of the Hawaiians,[14] and they have always been less than adequately represented in the occupations of commerce. The Part-Hawaiians have made a better adjustment here than the pure Hawaiians, although in 1950 the combined Hawaiian and Part-Hawaiian group was still markedly under-represented in managerial and proprietary occupations and as clerical and sales workers. This gap is gradually diminishing with the passage of time. On the other hand, the Hawaiians, and especially those of mixed ancestry, have re-

[13]It is obvious that representation in this field is partly a function of American education, in which the Filipinos are still somewhat handicapped. See *Supra*, Chapter 5. Quite clearly also the Filipinos are improving their position in both of these fields.
[14]Cf. Adams, *op. cit.*, pp. 243-246.

12. *EMPLOYED MALE CIVILIANS BY LARGER ETHNIC GROUPS AND MAJOR OCCUPATIONS, 1940, 1950,* 1960*

		ALL RACES		PER CENT OF TOTAL EMPLOYED				
		Number	Per Cent	Haw'n.	Cauca-sian	Chinese	Filipino	Japanese
Managers, Officials, and Proprietors, including Farm	1940	12,612	10.6	5.8	20.0	16.3	1.4	12.9
	1950	15,274	12.6	7.9	18.5	20.1	3.0	15.1
	1960	16,850	12.3		19.4	16.6	2.7	13.7
Clerical, Sales, and Kindred Workers	1940	12,371	10.4	8.3	16.3	28.6	1.6	11.4
	1950	15,049	12.4	9.9	14.1	26.3	3.4	15.1
	1960	17,149	12.5		13.3	21.3	4.8	14.8
Craftsmen, Foremen, and Kindred Workers	1940	15,526	13.0	15.4	17.4	10.2	2.4	18.8
	1950	25,251	20.9	22.9	21.2	18.4	7.5	27.7
	1960	32,312	23.6		19.2	20.7	14.3	30.2
Operatives and Kindred Workers	1940	14,422	12.1	19.8	14.4	12.0	8.0	11.6
	1950	19,350	16.0	20.1	12.7	11.3	19.9	15.0
	1960	20,687	15.2		11.7	9.9	22.1	13.0
Service Workers, including Household	1940	8,463	7.1	8.9	3.4	12.3	5.8	8.3
	1950	9,276	7.1	10.0	6.7	7.8	11.2	5.3
	1960	9,573	7.0		5.5	7.1	10.6	5.3

*The major occupational categories used in 1950 are not strictly comparable with those used in 1940, despite an obvious attempt by the census to secure comparability. Corrections have been made for the military population in the 1940 census returns by eliminating "soldiers, sailors, and marines," most of whom were Caucasians.

vealed a special aptitude as craftsmen of various sorts, including the operation and handling of machinery.

A major theme which runs through much of the data presented in this chapter has been the steady trend toward an equalization across ethnic lines of participation in the occupational life of the Islands. Obvious inequalities, based in part upon the order of arrival, the length of residence in Hawaii, and the cultural traditions which each group has perpetuated, still exist and will continue for some time in the future, but the differences become less apparent with each passing decade.[15] A single manifestation of this trend can be noted in the striking increase in the proportion of Filipinos as service workers and semi-skilled operators during the decade of the war, while at the same time the Chinese and to a lesser degree the Japanese moved out of these occupations to positions further up the economic scale. During the following decade, the broadening demand for craftsmen enabled Filipinos to make equally striking advances at this higher level. It is also evident, however, that the trends toward the equalization of occupational participation occur only in stages and usually involve a considerable number of separate steps. Some of the additional factors which affect the relative speed of the process will be indicated in the next chapter.

[15]A comparative study of the trend toward the equalization of occupational participation among Orientals in Hawaii and in continental United States indicates that the Chinese in Hawaii had advanced considerably further toward preferred positions than their kinsmen on the Mainland; the reverse was true of the Filipinos. The Japanese in Hawaii had surpassed their counterparts on the Mainland in commerce and trade and the skilled crafts, but had lagged somewhat behind in the professions.

5

WHAT ARE THEY BECOMING?

Hawaii's claim to distinction as a laboratory of race relations has been based upon the apparent ease with which peoples of sharply contrasted customs and life values have lived together and, to some extent, fused. Romanzo Adams concludes his *Peoples of Hawaii* with the observation that "Hawaii offers opportunity to the people of all races on terms that approach uncommonly close to equality. Responding to opportunity, the peoples are entering upon a larger social inheritance, and one may look forward to an enrichment of this heritage through the achievement of men and women of all races." To further test this hypothesis and to bring up to date some of the evidence presented by Adams on this theme will be the major objective of this concluding chapter.

EDUCATION AND ASSIMILATION

The prime requisite of an effective community involving peoples of diverse cultures is obviously free and easy communication among them. The distances which have separated the peoples and races of the world are, as Robert Park so insistently pointed out, not only physical and economic but also moral and social. In Hawaii, as truly as in continental United States, Brazil, India, or South Africa, the most refractory and vexing barriers to the creation of an integrated community in which all peoples participate have been man-made. The disposition to associate exclusively with one's own national or racial group and the corresponding rejection of persons outside that charmed circle are, of course, "in the minds of men." Our preferences and prejudices in matters of whom to marry, play, work, or worship with, as well as our other "ethnocentricities," obviously have to be learned; we are not born with them.

The fact that so many of Hawaii's residents have been born and nurtured outside the range of the Hawaiian and American social atmosphere is, of course, a limiting factor in the spiritual fusion or assimilation of the Island peoples. Hawaii's problem of making one people out of many has been greatly accentuated by the continuing presence of so many persons with but limited experience within the moral and political climate of the Islands. Obviously no simple barometer can be devised to measure the assimilative atmosphere which prevails, but the simple facts in Table 13 do provide something of a clue.

13. PERCENTAGE BORN OUTSIDE HAWAII OR MAINLAND UNITED STATES, 1896-1960

	1896	1910	1920	1930	1940	1950	1960
Portuguese	54.2	38.3	22.2	13.8	7.7	5.2	3.8
Other Caucasian	37.8	33.3	22.2	11.9			
Chinese	89.7	66.8	47.5	27.5	16.8	12.1	8.1
Japanese	91.5	75.0	55.5	34.7	23.7	15.8	11.3
Korean		92.0	70.4	46.2	35.8	25.2	
Filipino		99.8	89.0	83.5	68.1	55.7	41.7
Puerto Rican		71.8	46.1	32.7	22.3	12.3	
TOTAL POPULATION	49.2	51.9	42.4	33.5	21.3	15.2	10.9

The peak of Hawaii's flood of foreigners occurred between 1896 and 1910, with the highest proportion registered in the census of 1900 when 59 per cent of the population were recorded as foreign born. Since that date, each succeeding census has recorded a decline in the proportion of "outlanders," with the Caucasians—both Portuguese and Haoles—showing consistently the highest proportions of "native born." All the other immigrant groups have moved slowly but steadily toward a native-born population, with somewhat more than two generations in most cases being required to complete the process. We need not present here the reasons for the relative speed in the different groups —the somewhat slower pace of the Filipinos and the rather rapid pace of the Portuguese and Puerto Ricans. The statistics of Table 13 are provided rather as indicating the basic demographic limits upon assimilation in Hawaii.

Insofar as Hawaii has afforded a favorable atmosphere and setting for the free and equal participation by all its residents in the life of the community, it is the result not only of its limited area and the economic and occupational demands already discussed but also of the open channels of communication. The common language essential to such social interchange has been not Hawaiian, the indigenous tongue of the Islands, but English, the language of the invaders, or the makeshift language of the region, the so-called "pidgin English." The dominant role of the Yankee and British traders and missionaries in the trading centers established on each of the major islands during the first half of the nineteenth century gave to their language an advantage over all the competing tongues which were represented in these communities. Although it was the American missionaries who reduced the Hawaiian language to written form and most vigorously supported the practice of instructing the natives in the Hawaiian language,[1] their own use of the English language among themselves and with other foreigners served to give it special prestige. Thus, by the middle of the last century, English had become "the principal medium of business, government, and diplomacy" in the Islands, and considerable pressure was being exerted by Hawaiians "to have their children taught English in order to open to them wider avenues for advancement." [2] Beginning in 1844 a weekly newspaper, published in the English language, became the official organ of the government, and several additional journals began publication in English during the forties and fifties.

The Hawaiian language, quite naturally, continued to be the medium of communication among the natives themselves throughout the nineteenth century, but from the middle of the century increasing money and effort was expended upon the instruction of Hawaiian children in the English language. Commencing with ten English schools in 1854, the public school system of Hawaii was conducted increasingly in the language of the Haoles, such that all instruction was in English before the close of the century. The Protestant missionary emphasis upon the ability of their converts to read the Christian scriptures was unquestionably an important factor in the strong tradition of literacy

[1]It is difficult to appreciate the full significance of the intellectual transformation which occurred in Hawaii within little more than a decade. The missionary mentors were first required to learn the language itself, reduce it to written form, translate their message into Hawaiian, and publish textbooks, before they could even undertake the more difficult task of instructing the natives. Even more amazing is the fact that the Hawaiians should have participated with such enthusiasm in the venture of becoming almost overnight a literate people. Kuykendall reports that by 1831 or 1832 "the bulk of the adult population, certainly more than half, were taught to read, [and] many of them learned to write." Ralph S. Kuykendall, *The Hawaiian Kingdom, 1778-1854* (Honolulu: University of Hawaii Press, 1938), p. 109.

[2]*Ibid.*, p. 360.

which developed among the Hawaiian people. A high premium was also placed upon literacy by the Haoles, especially those in preferred positions, and the natives readily took over their values. In any case, the earliest reports in the Hawaiian census reveal a surprisingly high rate of literacy for the native population, considering the fact that they had so recently emerged from a preliterate culture.

14. PERCENTAGE OF POPULATION OF SCHOOL AGE OR OLDER WHO WERE LITERATE, 1890-1930

	AGE SIX AND OVER		AGE TEN AND OVER		
	1890	1896	1910	1920	1930
Hawaiian	79.8	84.0	95.3	97.0	96.6
Part-Hawaiian	83.1	91.2	98.6	99.2	99.3
Portuguese	29.4	27.8	74.6	81.1	90.3
Other Caucasian	91.4	85.7	96.5	99.2	99.7
Chinese	13.2	48.5	67.7	79.0	84.3
Japanese	2.5	53.6	65.0	79.2	87.3
Korean			74.1	82.7	82.4
Filipino			66.4	53.3	61.5
Puerto Rican			26.8	53.3	68.0
TOTAL POPULATION	48.9	63.9	73.2	81.1	84.9

According to the census of 1890, slightly more than four out of every five Hawaiians and Part-Hawaiians over the age of six were able to read and write, most of them still in the native tongue. This phenomenally high rate of literacy among the Hawaiians, exceeding that of all other ethnic groups except the Haoles, continued throughout the first three census periods of the twentieth century when such data were recorded. As one would expect, literacy has been consistently slightly higher among the Part-Hawaiians than among the pure Hawaiians, and in two of the five censuses, the rate of literacy among the Part-Hawaiians exceeded even that of the Haoles.[3]

Pronounced differences in the literacy of the immigrant groups, and especially in the speed with which improvement in literacy occurred

[3]A special investigation in 1896 revealed that 69 per cent of the Part-Hawaiians and 26 per cent of the pure Hawaiians over the age of six were able to read and write in the English language, as compared with 83 per cent of the Other Caucasians. Less than one-fourth of the total population were so qualified.

subsequently, are also apparent in the data of Table 14. The startling rise in the rates of literacy among the Chinese and Japanese between 1890 and 1896 is largely a matter of definition, the expression "able to read and write" having been confined in 1890 to "Hawaiian, English, or some European language only," whereas in 1896 apparently it applied to any language.[4] The relatively low rate of literacy among the Puerto Ricans as compared with the Koreans who arrived in Hawaii a few years later parallels the differences between the two groups noted in the previous chapter. In general the various immigrant groups have arrived in Hawaii with only a small proportion of their number able to read or write, but under the influence of American schools since Annexation, their rate of literacy has rapidly increased. Both the Koreans and the Filipinos have varied somewhat from this rule in that their ratios have been rather high almost from the outset. The failure of the census to record data on literacy after 1930 makes impossible any later comparisons, but it is reasonable to assume that much the same relative positions have been maintained.

It is commonly assumed that the ability to speak the English language provides a more accurate index of assimilation than the test of literacy usually applied by census enumerators, but there are sound reasons for doubting this assumption. It is unquestionably true that the acquiring of common sentiments, memories, and attitudes essential to assimilation involves ultimately the use of a common language; but there is considerable evidence that some of the most substantial steps in assimilation may take place while the immigrant is still almost wholly dependent upon his mother tongue. The obverse is equally true, viz., that the immigrant may learn the language of his adopted country without acquiring very much of its basic values and traditions.

Certainly the effective functioning of a modern democracy is dependent upon a citizenry which can read and write, as well as speak its language. At any rate, both the native Hawaiians and the various immigrants have, in general, moved more slowly in acquiring an ability to speak the English language than they have in becoming literate, although generally the same basic principles have applied. In 1910, for example, nearly three-fourths of the population of Hawaii ten years of age and older were reported as literate, but less than half of the same population were able to speak the English language. With the passing of the immigrant generation, quite naturally, the difference

[4]It should also be borne in mind that it was never possible to apply wholly adequate tests of literacy, and the returns, especially of the immigrant groups, are subject to some error.

between the two rates tends to diminish, and by 1930, 85 per cent were reported literate as compared with 75 per cent able to speak the English language. The Portuguese and Puerto Ricans have, in general, rated higher in ability to speak the language than in literacy, while the reverse has been true of the Chinese, Japanese, and Koreans.

The response to the opportunities for formal education reflects the interests and aspirations of the several ethnic groups, especially insofar as the values of the educational system are American and Western. Since the school system in Hawaii was inaugurated and directed during its early history by the Protestant missionaries from New England, it had from the outset a distinctly American orientation. Although the missionaries were at first opposed to the use of the English language, favoring Hawaiian as a means of preserving the native cultural values, they later gave full support to the use of English in the schools of Hawaii. Beginning in 1840, the youth of the Islands were increasingly drawn within the influence of the public schools, which supplemented the missionary schools already functioning. By the close of the century, the compulsory school attendance law was being efficiently enforced:

The system for enforcing the law for bringing children into school is peculiarly efficient in these islands. Very few children of school age escape being obliged to attend school. . . . There are very few countries . . . where education is so universal, and in a few decades, if things go on as they are now doing, there will be very few indeed who cannot read and write English. Those who are illiterate come to us from abroad.[5]

Allowing for possible errors in enumeration, the director of the census concluded that 81.8 per cent of the children of school age, then designated at six to fifteen years, were actually enrolled.

Following Annexation compulsory school attendance, with a completely American orientation, was even more rigorously enforced. No very pronounced differences between the various racial groups were discovered in the census reports covering compulsory school attendance except to indicate that there was a lower degree of conformity with the law in the case of the most recently arrived immigrants and in certain groups less impressed with the value of formal education.[6] A more sensitive indicator of differences in attitudes toward formal education in general and toward American education specifically is found in the proportion of children just beyond the compulsory school age who are actually attending school. Especially in the earlier decades

[5]*Report of the General Superintendent of the Census,* 1896. Honolulu, 1897, p. 100.
[6]Romanzo Adams, *The Peoples of Hawaii* (Honolulu: The Institute of Pacific Relations, 1935), p. 44.

of the present century, when industry and the press did not favor high school education for the masses, school attendance on the part of children aged sixteen or seventeen was chiefly a reflection of a strong educational urge on the part of the young people themselves and especially of their parents.

The tendency for the newly arrived immigrants to encourage their children to take employment as early as possible in order to assist in the economic support of the family is clearly evident in the relatively low rates of non-compulsory school attendance of the Japanese and

15. *PERCENTAGE OF 16- AND 17-YEAR-OLDS ATTENDING SCHOOL, 1910-1950*

	1910	1920	1930	1940	1950
Hawaiian	38.4	41.3	37.0	38.8 ⎫	
Part-Hawaiian	58.0	57.5	55.6	58.8 ⎬	78.1
Caucasian-Hawaiian	59.7	60.2	58.3		
Asiatic-Hawaiian	54.3	51.9	52.5		
Caucasian	25.9	34.0	49.1	58.6	77.4
Portuguese	15.5	25.8	35.6		
Other Caucasian	63.8	64.0	70.2		
Chinese	57.3	69.1	76.7	88.9	94.1
Japanese	29.9	35.1	54.3	72.8	94.1
Filipino	21.7	17.6	24.2	50.2	81.8
Korean	53.1	65.4	68.0		
Puerto Rican	8.4	9.3	15.2		
TOTAL POPULATION	35.9	40.1	51.4	67.1	85.8

Filipinos in 1910. This is, of course, consonant with the expectations of peasant peoples generally that children should sacrifice any personal ambitions for the welfare of the family. Among some of the peasant immigrants, such as the Portuguese and Puerto Ricans for example, one may also encounter an indifference to formal education, if not a positive suspicion of those seeking higher education as "putting on airs." On the other hand, the Chinese, Japanese, and Koreans, although of peasant origin, have also placed a high value upon scholarship, and the teacher and the learned person have enjoyed a place of dignity and prestige in the community. This fact, together with a growing recognition that education is indispensable to advancement on the economic and social scale in American society, are responsible for the rapid rise in the proportion of older Oriental children attending school. A pronounced tendency in Oriental families some decades ago to favor the boys in preference to the girls for such educational opportunities has now almost disappeared. Previous to 1940 the Chinese and Koreans enjoyed some advantage over the Japanese with reference to high school education, partly as a consequence of their residence in the urban centers, but by 1950 the rural areas were also well supplied with high schools.

Following Statehood, the unfortunate substitution of the Mainland color distinctions between White and Nonwhite instead of the usual Island ethnic categories prevents meaningful comparison with the earlier educational trends. The meager information available from a separate 1960 census bulletin on Nonwhite Population by Race indicates that in a 25 per cent sample of adults of Chinese and Japanese ancestry there had been a relatively slight increase over a decade in the median number of years of school completed, whereas among Filipinos, the increase had been quite considerable—between two and three years. In 1960 the median school years completed among Chinese and Japanese men and women, aged 25 to 34 years, was 12.5 years, with the Chinese men having a slightly higher median of 12.7 years. Among Filipinos of the same age, the median school years completed was 11.3 years among the men and 11.6 years among women. Chinese and Japanese men in Hawaii and both men and women among the Filipinos fell noticeably below their Mainland counterparts in the number of school years completed, whereas the women of Chinese and Japanese ancestry in the two areas were about on a par.

POLITICAL STATUS AND PARTICIPATION

The development of an effective political democracy is dependent upon the full and free participation of an informed citizenry in the basic decisions of the community. In a frontier region such as Hawaii, this entails not only a common language and education for the disparate peoples but also the creation of a common citizenry. During much of the last century, Hawaii's people were predominantly aliens or too young to enjoy the full privileges of citizenship. The story of the shifting political fortunes of the different ethnic groups during the second half of the nineteenth century is much too involved to consider here. In general, however, the plantation immigrant groups simply did not function in the political life of the community, and it was only after Annexation that the burgeoning immigrant peoples began to figure at all in the emerging democracy of the Islands.

16. PERCENTAGE OF POPULATION 21 YEARS OF AGE AND OVER WHO WERE CITIZENS, 1910-1950*

	1910†	1930‡	1950§
Hawaiian and Part-Hawaiian	99.2	99.8	99.0
Portuguese	40.4	77.6 ⎫	63.9
Other Caucasian	76.7	50.1 ⎭	
Chinese	5.9	45.5	82.1
Japanese	.2	16.0	70.8
Filipino			14.9
TOTAL POPULATION	24.7	37.1	65.7

*Data for smaller groups have not been listed separately. Comparable data for 1960 not available.
†Based on male population only.
‡Based on Adams, *People of Hawaii*, p. 16.
§Based on Territorial citizenship, which implies residence in the Territory for at least a year and hence excludes most of the armed forces.

Hawaii was annexed as a Territory of the United States under an Organic Act and laws which its people as a whole did not help to formulate. The federal laws relating to citizenship arbitrarily excluded from political participation all of the Chinese, Japanese, Korean, and Filipino immigrants, who together constituted three-quarters of the population 21 years of age and over in 1900. As a consequence, it has been impossible to apply in Hawaii the test of assimilation frequently utilized, viz., the extent to which the immigrants have applied for American citizenship. Only a handful of Orientals already citizens of the Republic of Hawaii were granted American citizenship when Hawaii was annexed, and although the immigrant children born in Hawaii after 1898 were American citizens, the number who were old enough to exercise the full rights of citizenship prior to 1920 was very small.

One can immediately recognize in the data on citizenship in 1910 the basis for part of Ray Stannard Baker's widely heralded statement that he had never seen a region with "so much philanthropy and so little democracy." Within the short space of forty years, however, the situation had been completely altered, so that the population of Oriental ancestry who were formerly almost excluded from participation in the affairs of government are now more favorably situated than even the Caucasians to exercise at least the minimum rights of citizenship. The proportion of the Haole group eligible to take part in local government had notably declined during the first half of the present century owing to the large number engaged in military defense and hence unable to meet the minimum residence requirement.

Nowhere else under the American flag has there been an experiment in political democracy involving such a large proportion of voters of Oriental ancestry, and quite naturally it has been watched with utmost interest by residents of the Islands, as well as outsiders. Many supposedly competent observers have speculated as to the probable outcome of this venture and have sometimes arrived at distinctly pessimistic conclusions. Because of the large proportion of Japanese in the total population, many of the predictions regarding the success or failure of the enterprise have focused around this one ethnic group. An acting governor of the Territory informed the President of the United States in 1907 that:

There is no narrow race prejudice in fairly facing and acknowledging the fact that the Oriental and the White can never labor side by side; and it is only political prudence to realize in time that neither laws nor education can make the Asiatic fit to enter an American voting booth. In our islands we see a growing generation who accept our public schools and all the other benefits of our institutions but lose none of their loyalty to the alien land of their forefathers. Hawaii presents the anomaly never dreamed of by any founders of our republic, of a land under the American flag in which the dominant sentiment is loyalty to a foreign emperor.

A group of prominent educators from continental United States in 1920 gave major attention in their report on education in Hawaii to the alleged rapid expansion of the local electorate of Japanese ancestry:

By 1930, it seems probable that the Japanese may comprise about 28 per cent of the electorate, a sufficiently large proportion to constitute a force that must be reckoned with if it acts as a unit. By 1940 about 47 per cent of the electorate may be expected to be composed of voters of this race. From this time on, their numerical superiority will grow rapidly, the voters doubling every 21 years, as children of children enter the electorate.[7]

The story of what has actually happened with regard to the potential voting strength of the different racial groups is partially told in the following table.

One of the most striking facts revealed in Table 17 is the rapidly broadening of the base of Hawaii's political structure, which increased

[7]U.S. Bureau of Education, *A Survey of Education in Hawaii*, Bulletin 16 (1920), p. 20.

nearly nine times between 1910 and 1950, the last census in which such data are recorded. The very pronounced decline in the potential political strength of the Hawaiians along with an equally striking rise in the voting power of the Japanese, in what appears like the displacement by a relatively new immigrant group of the established native population from its long established and preferred position, has not occurred without some tension. Although the expansive phase in the coming of age among the second generation citizens of Japanese ancestry has passed its prime, this group, by virtue of its size, is likely to be viewed with some concern by those who are critical of the Hawaiian experiment in political democracy. Charges that the voters of Japanese ancestry will combine their forces on critical issues, that they will throw their entire numerical strength behind Japanese candidates, and that the control of the government of Hawaii will ultimately gravitate into their hands—such are the allegations which are repeated privately by some disappointed Islanders and publicly by disapproving outsiders. The fact that such allegations have not and cannot be substantiated does not, of course, prevent their being circulated.

17. *PERCENTAGE DISTRIBUTION BY RACE OF ADULT CITIZEN POPULATION, 1910-1950*

	1910*	1930†	1950
Hawaiian and Part-Hawaiian	47.5	26.8	18.5
Portuguese	9.6	12.2	25.4
Other Caucasian	25.4	36.9	
Chinese	3.9	8.0	8.6
Japanese	.4	12.0	40.2
Korean		.3	
Filipino			3.0
Puerto Rican	7.5	3.5	
TOTAL NUMBER	20,748	81,079	189,616

*1910 figures include only the male citizens 21 years of age and over.
†Based on Adams, *Peoples of Hawaii*, p. 16.

The concern regarding racial bloc voting becomes even more acute when attention is focused exclusively on the number and ratio of voters by ancestry. The decision by Territorial officials in 1940 not to continue keeping records of the racial ancestry of the registered voters, as being out of keeping with democratic principles, makes it impossible to document precisely what has happened in this area since that time and thus effectively to controvert irresponsible assertions regarding the voting strength of the various ethnic groups. The data in Table 18 does indicate, however, that the Hawaiians and Part-Hawaiians were the only ethnic group during the first forty years after Annexation with a sufficient proportion of voters even to consider ethnic bloc voting as an effective device for controlling an election covering the entire Territory, and this held true only until about 1925. In the light of developments since that time, the prospects are slight indeed that a majority of the voters of all the islands would in the foreseeable future be confined to a single ethnic group. What is more important, however, is that even in a local election district, where a majority of the voters might be of the candidate's own ethnic group, publicly to solicit support on a racial basis would under Hawaiian conditions be tantamount to committing political suicide. The candidate would draw to himself the wrath of all the other ethnic groups as well as the hostility of the members of his own group in the opposition party.

The data in Table 18 further support the impression of an emerging electorate which is much more representative of the Island citizenry than was true at the beginning of the century. They do not support the impression that any one of the ethnic groups was securing even numerical control of the Hawaiian electorate.

PLANE OF LIVING

One of the most common bases of criticism of immigrant groups and an alleged evidence of their nonassimilation is their supposed failure to relinquish the customs and habits of the homeland. More specifically, it is charged that the immigrants are content to live on the meager standards of food, clothing, housing, and recreation of their homeland; that they are willing to work long hours at low pay; and that consequently they undermine the higher standards in the country to which they have migrated. This conception of the immigrant provides a justification both to the employer, for keeping wages at a low level on grounds that "foreigners can't use more money and any excess will only be sent back to the old country," and to the workers, for urging exclusion from the country, from labor unions, and from the neighborhood.

The experience of immigrant labor groups in Hawaii has conformed to this general conception, particularly in the early period of residence in the Islands. On arrival in Hawaii, they have preferred the familiar ways of life of the homeland, as well as the company of their com-

18. REGISTERED VOTERS, 1902-1940

	NUMBER OF VOTERS					PER CENT OF TOTAL				
	1902	1910	1920	1930	1940	1902	1910	1920	1930	1940
Hawaiian and Part-Hawaiian	8,680	9,619	14,650	19,858	21,581	68.8	66.6	55.6	38.1	24.7
Portuguese	594	1,530	3,091	8,111 ⎫	26,322	4.7	10.6	11.7	15.8 ⎫	30.1
Other Caucasian	3,192	2,884	6,795	12,158 ⎭		25.3	20.0	25.8	23.3 ⎭	
Chinese	143	396	1,141	4,402	7,422	1.1	2.7	4.3	8.4	8.5
Japanese	3	13	658	7,017	27,107	.0	.1	2.5	13.4	31.0
All Others				603	4,880				1.0	5.6
TOTAL	12,612	14,442	26,335	52,149	87,312	100.0	100.0	100.0	100.0	100.0

patriots in the strange land of exile; and they have, in general, been willing to work hard and long to accumulate some savings for their kinfolk at home. The transformation of the immigrants from sojourners in a strange and alien land to permanent and enthusiastic participants in the life of their adopted land obviously requires time and, of course, for many of the immigrants, their own lifetime is not sufficient. Several tangible and verifiable pieces of evidence that a change of this type has occurred or is now taking place among the immigrants to Hawaii are available.

Insofar as success in the Western world is measured by monetary standards, the assimilation of the immigrants can be partially gauged by their effectiveness in accumulating wealth. It is true, of course, that most of the immigrants to Hawaii were drawn to the Islands by the hope of winning a fortune so as to advance their status at home; but few of them had any experience in the game as played by Western rules. Obviously not all of the immigrants have been successful in this competition, but any who did succeed had to "play lightly" with many of their old-country moral and cultural values which did not fit in with the new rules of the game. The acquisition of the necessary skills for effective competition has evidently been considerably easier for most of the immigrants and their children than for the native Hawaiians, and there is some evidence that immigrants from China, Korea, and Japan, perhaps in that order, have enjoyed some advantage over the Portuguese, Puerto Ricans, or Filipino immigrants by virtue of the cultural traditions which they brought with them.

Records of local bank deposits, which are available from 1910 to 1934, reveal steadily mounting per capita figures for the three larger immigrant groups.[8] The Japanese per capita savings in Hawaii for example, increased from $2.40 in 1910 to $64.83 in 1930, with a decline thereafter to $54.57 in 1934, owing to the effects of the depression. Their savings in Hawaiian banks were relatively inconsequential until late in the twenties, most of their earnings prior to that time having been used to meet current expenses or to assist relatives in Japan. The figure for the Chinese was $13.35 in 1910 which increased to $153.01 in 1925, while the per capita savings among the Portuguese rose from $40.85 in 1910 to a peak of $130.54 in 1932.

Per capita valuations of real estate and personal property taxed by the Territory of Hawaii indicate a similar investment of savings by the immigrants. The per capita assessed valuation on personal property

[8]Andrew W. Lind, *An Island Community* (Chicago: University of Chicago Press, 1938), pp. 265-267.

owned by Portuguese rose from $21.44 in 1911 to $53.69 in 1930 and on real estate from $105.80 to $522.62 in the same period. Comparable increases occurred in the valuation of real estate owned by the Chinese and the Japanese, except that the valuation in both cases was considerably lower in 1911 and for the Chinese it rose somewhat higher ($570.26) by 1930. "The Orientals have been somewhat slower in their accumulation of real property than have the Portuguese and Hawaiians, but as their hopes of retirement in the homeland diminish and as farm lands become available, the Chinese and Japanese investments mount rapidly." [9] Unfortunately, similar data are not available for the last three decades, but all the evidence points to much larger and more uniformly distributed investments among all the ethnic groups, especially since World War II.

Census data available for 1949 and for four of the larger groups in 1959 indicate that the sharp distinctions which once existed between the average incomes of the several ethnic groups are much less clearly drawn than formerly. They show, moreover, that one of the immigrant groups which was once concentrated at the bottom rung of the economic ladder is now well represented at the top levels, with an average income above that of any other group. Table 19 reveals that the Chinese males had by 1950 succeeded so well in the economic struggle that their median annual income exceeded that of their nearest rivals, the Caucasians, by $108, and by 1959 this differential had increased to $1,447. The median income of Japanese males, despite their shorter period of experience in the Island economic scene, was in 1949 significantly above that of the Hawaiians, although still notably below that of the Caucasians.

The relatively slow economic advancement of the Hawaiians as compared with the major immigrant groups reflects the persistence of traditional values, in which the accumulation of money and the character traits essential to it do not figure too prominently. Although their median income in 1949 was slightly above that recorded for all males, the proportion of Hawaiians and Part-Hawaiians in the lowest income class was notably above that of any of the major immigrant groups. Other evidence indicates that the pure Hawaiians, even more disproportionately than the Part-Hawaiians, were represented in the bottom income level, and that the economic handicap of both Hawaiians and Part-Hawaiians continues down to the present.

The relatively low income level of the Filipinos both in 1949 and 1959 is a function of several factors—their late arrival in the Islands as com-

9Ibid., p. 267.

19. PERCENTAGE OF MALES RECEIVING INCOMES IN 1949, 1959 BY INCOME CLASSES

	Up to $999	$1,000-1,999	$2,000-2,999	$3,000-3,999	$4,000-4,999	$5,000-6,999	$7,000-9,999	$10,000 and Over	Median Income
All Races									
1949	16.6	22.3	27.1	17.6	6.9	5.3	2.1	1.8	$2,340
1959	11.3	14.4	12.2	16.0	13.0	18.0	8.7	6.5	3,717
Caucasian									
1949	9.7	24.8	17.8	18.3	10.1	11.0	4.6	3.7	2,856
1959	7.9	21.5	11.9	12.7	10.9	14.5	9.9	10.6	3,649
Chinese									
1949	17.6	14.9	20.2	22.9	11.9	7.5	3.4	3.5	2,964
1959	10.8	7.0	6.9	10.2	13.7	26.1	15.4	9.8	5,096
Japanese									
1949	17.5	17.3	29.6	21.1	6.8	3.7	1.4	1.5	2,427
1959	12.5	8.4	8.9	15.4	15.8	24.2	9.7	5.0	4,302
Filipino									
1949	18.1	32.6	40.2	7.6	1.2	.5	.1	.1	1,995
1959	14.5	11.6	22.0	28.0	11.7	9.5	2.3	.5	3,071
Hawaiian and Part-Hawaiian									
1949	22.5	17.2	25.5	21.5	7.1	3.7	1.5	.7	2,369

pared with other immigrant groups, the high sex disproportion and the consequent lack of a stable family life, and possibly also less experience in a competitive trading economy.

The limited data available for 1959 indicate a mounting affluence in which presumably all the ethnic groups shared. Among the notable changes during the preceding decade was the very much higher rate of increase in median incomes among the Japanese and Chinese as compared with the Caucasians. The inclusion of Puerto Ricans in the census category of Caucasians in 1959 had the effect of lowering somewhat the combined level. At both the 1949 and 1959 census periods the Caucasians and the Chinese had a disproportionate percentage in the highest income class, less so in 1959, and with the passage of time, the differences between the various groups are gradually diminishing.

Early marriage and large families are commonly accepted social values in most of the peasant and folk societies from which Hawaii's immigrant and indigenous peoples have been drawn. Consequently the postponement of marriage and the restriction of family size have come to be regarded as evidences of the assimilation of these groups into American life. Other factors, such as the availability of women and the economic level of the group, also play a part in determining the age at marriage and the size of the family, and it is therefore necessary to use these indices with some caution. In general, however, the newly arrived immigrant groups and the native Hawaiian population tend to marry early, insofar as women are available, and to have relatively large families. As they absorb the customs and ideals of the developing American community in Hawaii, the men in each of the immigrant groups become conscious of the community pressure to establish themselves economically and professionally before entering into marriage. The pressure to postpone marriage and to restrict the number of children within the family naturally operates more effectively upon the second generation than upon their immigrant parents; and there is therefore something of a time lag until the secularizing influences of the American community take effect.

Owing to the scarcity of women in most of the immigrant groups a generation ago, many of the younger men were unable to secure wives, even if they wished to. Hence the proportion of younger women who were married affords a better index of the persistence of peasant or folk traditions than the same ratio of men. There was in 1920 an almost perfect inverse correlation between the proportion of married women aged fifteen to twenty-four in the different immigrant groups and the length of their residence in Hawaii. On this basis it would

appear that the Chinese were somewhat more Americanized or Westernized in 1920 than the Portuguese, who had arrived in the Territory at about the same time. It would also appear, as one would
expect, that the Part-Hawaiians had been more affected by Western
values than had the pure Hawaiians.

20. *PERCENTAGES OF MEN AND WOMEN 15-24 YEARS OLD
WHO WERE MARRIED, 1920, 1950, 1960*

	MARRIED MEN			MARRIED WOMEN		
	1920	1950	1960*	1920	1950	1960*
All Races	12.3	11.7	16.8	52.3	30.0	35.3
Hawaiian	18.8 ⎫ 15.1			51.7 ⎫ 36.4		
Part-Hawaiian	16.0 ⎭			35.6 ⎭		
Portuguese	14.8 ⎫ 14.3		22.2	44.1 ⎫ 51.2		55.8
Other Caucasian	5.5 ⎭			34.2 ⎭		
Chinese	11.4	10.5	7.4	38.0	24.7	18.1
Japanese	10.8	6.5	8.6	58.5	18.2	18.7
*Korean**	15.3	14.5		83.4	29.5	
*Puerto Rican**	21.0	20.2		63.1	41.2	
Filipino	13.6	14.9	16.8	90.0	40.8	40.8

*Figures for Hawaiian, Part-Hawaiian, Korean, and Puerto Rican not separately
available.

Insofar as comparable data were available for 1950 and 1960, the
general ranking of the various groups continued to be the same, except
that the Caucasian group—influenced strongly by the Portuguese and
the military components—now had the highest ratio married among
their young adult women. Considering the high over-proportion of
young adult males, especially among the Caucasian military, it is not
surprising that the available women of like age should be under
pressure to marry early. That the Caucasian males should also in
1960 have shown a higher tendency toward early marriage than the
other ethnic groups in Hawaii is in part a reflection of a similar fashion
trend on the Mainland. On the other hand, there is a strong suggestion
that the trend toward earlier marriage noted throughout the population of both sexes between 1950 and 1960 may also have been significantly influenced by the widespread and mounting affluence of this
period. The one exception noted in Table 20 is found among the

Chinese, whose rate of early marriage continued to drop steadily among both sexes.

BIRTHS AND DEATHS AS ASSIMILATIVE INDICES

The conscious restriction of family size, which is so commonly identified with the efforts of people to improve their economic and social position, presupposes a higher degree of education in Western values and a greater emancipation from old country traditions than can be expected of the first generation immigrants. One discovers therefore consistently high birth rates and larger families on the part of the immigrants. These persist for some years after the close of immigration, and the pronounced changes do not occur until the second generation arrives at the childbearing age. In the absence of accurate records on births for an extended period during and following immigration, the simple ratio of children under the age of five for every thousand women of childbearing age provides a simple and reasonably accurate measure of fertility.

21. CHILDREN UNDER FIVE YEARS OF AGE PER THOUSAND WOMEN AGED 20-44, 1910-1960

	1910	1920	1930	1940	1950	1960
All Races	837	957	991	606	696	738
Hawaiian and Part-Hawaiian	802	945	1,091	1,014	1,144	1,154
Portuguese	1,207	1,138	673 ⎫	362	541	709
Other Caucasian	535	352	441 ⎭			
Chinese	1,191	1,285	982	421	596	629
Japanese	735	964	1,112	550	567	521
Korean	1,105	1,405	1,375		683	
Filipino		960	1,429	1,411	1,293	1,155
Puerto Rican	1,374	1,329	1,112		938	

The biologically expansive effect of the frontier situation does not reflect itself immediately after immigration upon the number of children under the age of five, partly because of the heavy toll of infant deaths in the immigrant groups. Thus the maximum rate of biological expansion in the Territory did not occur until 1930, although the rate was high throughout the three previous decades.

Most impressive, however, is the regular and consistent manner in which the ratio of young children in each immigrant group tapers off as the group begins to improve its plane of living according to Western standards. This decline was especially evident for the Chinese and Japanese between 1930 and 1940, but during the following decade Hawaii obviously shared in the wartime population boom, with fertility ratios mounting for all ethnic groups, except the Filipinos. As the latest arrivals whose peasant tradition measures wealth in the number of one's offspring, their fertility ratio was so inordinately high in both 1930 and 1940 that it could only decline, as it continued to do for another twenty years. The postwar baby-boom continued into the 1950's for the Hawaiians, Caucasians, and Chinese, but obviously disappeared among the Japanese whose 1960 fertility ratio was lower than before the war.

Ordinary birth rates, in a region where the number of males so greatly exceeds the females, afford no accurate indication of either fertility or the plane of living. A corrected birth rate, based not on the total population, but on the critical population of women of the childbearing years, confirms the story already told of immigrant groups responding to a mounting plane of living by restricting their births.

Again we discover that it is the most recently arrived immigrant groups which have the highest general fertility rates owing to the restraining influences of the American environment upon the fertility of the groups which arrived earlier. Except for the postwar period, the longer the groups have remained in Hawaii, the lower their fertility.

This is no less true of the Japanese than of the Portuguese or Filipinos. The religious injunctions of the Old World to "reproduce and multiply the earth" have apparently not been able to withstand the secularizing influence of the West. The low fertility of Other Caucasian women in 1932 was a reflection of their middle- and upper-class status and it was somewhat approximated by the Chinese and Japanese groups in 1940.

The increase in the general fertility rates of all the major groups except the Filipinos between 1940 and 1950 corresponds, of course, with the experience in continental United States and probably represents only a temporary reversal of the downward trend, as the limited data for 1960 clearly suggest. Although the rate for the entire population had increased slightly in the preceding decade, it was chiefly confined to the Hawaiian and Caucasian groups, the latter being artificially augmented by the influx of young military wives at the optimum age of child-bearing. The rate among the Chinese, Filipino, and Japanese groups declined substantially, for the latter group to a point below that of 1940 and the lowest of any of the major ethnic groups. This is all the more significant in the light of the dire predictions prior to the war about the "Yellow Peril" and the "overly fecund" Japanese.

22. BIRTHS PER THOUSAND WOMEN 15-44 YEARS OLD, 1932-1960*

	1932†	1940‡	1950‡	1960
All Races	169	107	128	130
Hawaiian and Part-Hawaiian	187	166	167	181
Portuguese	140 ⎫	87	126	141
Other Caucasian	79 ⎭			
Chinese	139	78	116	92
Japanese	170	90	102	86
Koreans§	180			
Filipino	312	192	193	185
Puerto Rican§	218			

*Racial classification is that of mother and not necessarily child.
†Based on Adams, *Peoples of Hawaii*, p. 22.
‡Number of births used in computation is the average for three years, including the year preceding and the year following.
§Figures only for 1932.

Although a declining death rate is also associated with a mounting plane of living in accordance with Western standards, the peculiar circumstances of population distribution in Hawaii make it difficult to secure accurate and meaningful indices. Hawaii's population is still made up disproportionately of young people, whose death rate should be low. Moreover, many of the older immigrants have gone back to their homeland to die. Infant mortality, on the other hand, can be more accurately computed and is perhaps one of the best "indices of civilization" and of acculturation in an immigrant situation.

The extraordinary decline in the rate of mortality per thousand babies from 119 in 1924 to 21 in 1960 is all the more impressive when compared with rates for continental United States of 71 and 25 respectively. Throughout the period for which data are available, the pure Hawaiians present the least favorable picture of all, suggesting the survival of customs relating to birth and infant care which are inappropriate under modern conditions, however adequate they may have been when the natives lived in isolation. In contrast to the unmixed Hawaiians have been the Filipinos, whose 1924 mortality rate of more than one child out of every four, resulting also from antiquated folk beliefs in evil spirits and superstitious practices, had been reduced in 1963 to one death out of every fifty births. The uniformly low rates in recent years for all groups except the Hawaiians is largely a testimony to the effective public health program in the Islands.

23. DEATHS UNDER ONE YEAR OF AGE PER THOUSAND BIRTHS, 1924-1963

	1924	1929	1940	1950	1960	1963
All Races	119	91	50	24	22	21
Hawaiian	285	198	129	60	42	38
Part-Hawaiian	96	109	57	26	26	25
Portuguese	100	64 }	39	24	20	20
Other Caucasian	44	49 }				
Chinese	64	55	40	24	21	21
Japanese	88	57	34	18	22	17
Korean	70	51	36	19	29	16
Filipino	296	219	73	31	25	22
Puerto Rican	110	99	67	26	24	13

ONE PEOPLE OUT OF MANY

The ultimate test of the social and spiritual fusion of the peoples in any area where diverse ethnic groups have been brought together is their loss of any sense of significant differences among them. When Chinese, Haoles, Hawaiians, Japanese, and Puerto Ricans have become accustomed to carrying on together the activities of life that matter to all without any awareness that they are Chinese, Haoles, Hawaiians, Japanese, or Puerto Ricans, one could say that the process of assimilation was complete. Quite obviously this is a protracted and involved process for which there can be no single, unitary index. Some indicators of this process have already been examined in this and previous chapters. There remains to be considered what is perhaps the ultimate criterion of intimacy in interethnic relations, at least under the American rules of the game, marriage.

The fact that marriage across racial lines has always been legally sanctioned in Hawaii may be interpreted merely as evidence of a basic tolerance, whose positive nature is reflected only in the actual practice of securing marriage mates without regard to ethnic lines. As long as any ethnic group continues to be highly conscious of itself as distinct from all others and as the guardians of a unique and valued tradition, strenuous efforts will be made to discourage its members from marrying outside the group. Insofar as the ethnocentric influence is sustained, it registers in a low outmarriage rate. With the decline of group consciousness and ethnocentrism, whatever the factors contributing to this may be, the selection of a mate from within the group ceases to figure so prominently in the choice and the rate of outmarriage is likely to mount.

Accurate statistics of this phenomenon are available for most of the period since 1912, and they provide a clear and vivid account of the slow but steady process by which the many races of Hawaii are losing their separate identities and are becoming one. Depending upon the date at which one begins his computations and the racial definitions then in vogue, one arrives at different conclusions as to the extent of interracial marriage, but all the evidences point to a distinct increase over a fifty-year period. Romanzo Adams, utilizing the twelvefold racial classification common in Hawaii in 1937, observed that while 13 per cent of the marriages in 1912-1913 were interracial in character, by 1931-1932 the ratio had increased to 32 per cent. During the period of World War II (1942-1944), the marriages across these twelve race lines constituted 38.5 per cent of all marriages.

So extensive had marriage between the two types of Part-Hawaiians and between the Portuguese, Spanish, and Other Caucasians become that the census in 1940 abandoned these separate designations. The Territorial Bureau of Vital Statistics followed the same procedure later in the same decade, with the result that only eight racial groups are included in the table indicating the rates of interracial marriage for the entire 1912-1964 period.

The very pronounced sex disproportions in the case of the Chinese, Filipinos, Koreans, and Caucasians had the effect of accentuating the rate of outmarriage of the men and of greatly retarding that of the women in these groups. The excess of males in these groups also placed a premium upon the women of the other groups, with the

24. INTERRACIAL MARRIAGES AS PERCENTAGE OF ALL MARRIAGES, 1912-1964

		TOTAL NUMBER OF MARRIAGES						PER CENT OUTMARRIAGES					
		1912-1916*	1920-1930*	1930-1940	1940-1949‡	1950-1959‡	1960-1964‡	1912-1916*	1920-1930*	1930-1940	1940-1949‡	1950-1959‡	1960-1964‡
Hawaiian	Grooms	1,018	1,972	1,459	1,137	965	391	19.4	33.3	55.2	66.3	78.9	85.9
	Brides	1,366	2,748	1,751	1,682	1,091	379	39.9	52.1	62.7	77.2	81.5	85.4
Part-Hawaiian	Grooms	455	2,164	3,567	5,142	7,502	4,766	52.1	38.8	41.0	36.9	41.3	47.0
	Brides	645	3,133	5,001	8,147	10,583	5,885	66.2	57.7	57.9	64.2	58.4	56.8
Caucasian	Grooms	2,297	7,301	9,921	19,887	17,848	10,343	17.3	24.3	22.4	33.8	37.4	35.1
	Brides	2,151	6,408	8,893	14,670	13,360	8,518	11.7	13.8	10.7	10.2	16.4	21.1
Chinese	Grooms	480	1,617	1,956	2,865	2,641	1,101	41.7	24.8	28.0	31.2	43.6	54.8
	Brides	297	1,442	1,969	3,176	2,717	1,147	5.7	15.7	28.5	38.0	45.2	56.6
Japanese	Grooms	6,395	8,261	10,114	14,680	15,509	6,199	0.5	2.7	4.3	4.3	8.7	15.7
	Brides	6,376	8,301	10,331	16,909	17,498	7,009	0.2	3.1	6.3	16.9	19.1	25.4
Korean	Grooms	267	443	412	687	632	301	26.4	17.6	23.5	49.0	70.3	77.1
	Brides	196	384	516	1,055	736	347	0.0	4.9	39.0	66.7	74.5	80.1
Filipino	Grooms	684	3,355	3,593	5,092	6,108	3,095	21.8	25.6	37.5	42.0	44.5	51.2
	Brides	550	2,522	2,339	3,738	5,282	2,876	2.8	1.0	4.0	21.0	35.8	47.5
Puerto Rican	Grooms	197	706	677	1,138	1,147	559	24.4	18.6	29.8	39.5	51.3	65.0
	Brides	203	953	873	1,385	1,415	589	26.4	39.7	42.8	50.3	60.5	67.2
TOTAL		11,826	26,090	31,863	51,140	53,344	27,559	11.5	19.2	22.8	28.6	32.8	37.6

*Derived from Romanzo Adams, *Interracial Marriage in Hawaii*, pp. 336-339.
†Bureau of Vital Statistics, July 1, 1940-June 30, 1948 and calendar year 1949.
‡Bureau of Health Statistics, calendar years 1950-1963.

result that a considerably smaller number of Japanese, Hawaiian, Part-Hawaiian, and Puerto Rican men than women were able to secure marriage mates. The artificial stimulation of outmarriage by an excess of adult males over females had largely ceased in the case of the Koreans and the Chinese before 1930, but it has continued among the Caucasians and the Filipinos until the present. Thus there was a temporary decline in the proportion of outmarriages of the Korean and Chinese men as the supply of women from their own groups gradually increased, but since 1930 there has been an increase in the outmarriage ratio of both sexes—phenomenally so in the case of the Koreans—as the pressure of old-country values has declined.

The war, with its large influx of Mainland defense workers and service personnel, had the effect of accelerating the outmarriage especially of Caucasian males and non-Caucasian females. It is also noticeable, however, that during the war decade the males in all the ethnic groups other than the Part-Hawaiians and Japanese found their wives increasingly outside their own ethnic group. The common assumption that the undermining influence of the war upon racial ties was only temporary and that there would be a postwar recession in the outmarriage rate has not been borne out by the subsequent experience. On the contrary, all the ethnic groups, with the exception of the Part-Hawaiian women and the Caucasian men, revealed steadily increasing outmarriage rates during the eighteen years immediately following the war. Even the Japanese, whose large numbers and cultural traditions have encouraged inmarriage to a greater degree than in any other ethnic group, have decidedly higher outmarriage rates during the 1950's and 1960's than ever before.

To examine in any detail the direction in which the various ethnic groups have turned for their exogamous partners, much less to determine the complex bases for their choices, is a task far beyond the scope of this study, but a few meaningful generalizations may be derived from a simple statistical summary of the marriages according to the race of both brides and grooms (Table 25). What is immediately apparent is the presence during the five-year period of all except two of the possible eighty-one different combinations of ethnic groups, large or small, and instances of these two missing combinations, involving smaller ethnic groups, have appeared in the record numerous times before. The wide catholicity in the marriage choices of both Hawaiians and Part-Hawaiians is evident, with an understandable tendency of Hawaiian men to marry Part-Hawaiian women in disproportionate numbers. There is a strong suggestion of greater selec-

25. *MARRIAGES BY RACE OF GROOM AND RACE OF BRIDE, 1960-1964*

GROOM	BRIDE										
	Caucasian	Hawaiian	Part-Hawaiian	Chinese	Filipino	Japanese	Puerto Rican	Korean	Other Races	TOTAL	PER CENT OUT-MARRIAGES
Caucasian	6,717	87	1,551	203	630	654	174	98	229	10,343	35.1
Hawaiian	71	55	213	8	19	12	6	2	5	391	85.9
Part-Hawaiian	868	133	2,526	177	405	441	101	53	62	4,766	47.0
Chinese	112	3	132	498	39	285	2	24	6	1,101	54.8
Filipino	298	62	722	49	1,510	236	74	22	122	3,095	51.2
Japanese	213	13	344	169	139	5,226	18	72	5	6,199	15.7
Puerto Ricans	92	9	144	9	65	24	193	4	11	551	65.0
Korean	36	2	35	25	20	114		69		301	77.1
Other Races	111	15	188	9	50	17	20	3	399	812	50.9
TOTAL	8,518	379	5,855	1,147	2,876	7,009	589	347	839	27,559	
Per Cent Outmarriages	21.1	85.4	56.8	56.6	47.5	25.4	67.2	80.1	52.4		37.6

tivity in the choice of out-group marriage mates, especially among the men of ethnic groups with strong and highly formalized family traditions, such as the Chinese and Japanese and even the Caucasians. The Koreans, by virtue of their limited numbers, are unable to impose their traditional definitions of marriage selection, which correspond in many essentials to those of the Japanese and Chinese, with anything like the same effectiveness, and hence individual choice operates much more extensively among both men and women. It is probable, as Adams deduced from evidence of an earlier period, that their common Roman Catholic religion has contributed to the considerable intermarriage among the Filipinos, Puerto Ricans, and the Portuguese included in the Caucasian group.

A final word of caution in the interpretation of the data in Table 25 is required. It must be remembered that marriages involve a preference and a consent of at least two and usually more different parties and that the resulting choices are further influenced by a variety of factors, including the size, social status, territorial distribution, age and sex disproportions, and the familial traditions among the ethnic groups involved.

A corollary interest in interracial marriage as an index of the assimilation of Hawaii's several ethnic groups naturally relates to the stability of interracial marriages as compared with intraracial marriages. The common assumption that marriages across ethnic lines, by virtue of the greater hazards resulting from deeply rooted differences in customs and values, necessarily result in higher divorce rates seems to have been validated by Hawaii's earlier experience. Adams' analysis of marriage and divorce records in 1927 indicated that the ratio of divorced persons was significantly lower among the inmarried of all races than among the outmarried and that "divorce rates are highest among . . . the members of the racial groups that outmarry the most." [10] A later study based upon Hawaii's experience between 1956 and 1962 reveals that although the rate of divorce was still somewhat higher among outmarried couples than among inmarried couples, the difference between them was greatly reduced over the span of thirty years and that "among five of Hawaii's nine major ethnic groups—all with divorce rates above the average—family breakdown was significantly less among those who had married out than among those who found marriage mates within the ethnic group." [11] Even

[10]Romanzo Adams, *Interracial Marriage in Hawaii* (New York: The Macmillan Company, 1937), p. 225.

[11]Andrew W. Lind, "Interracial Marriage as Affecting Divorce in Hawaii," *Sociology and Social Research*, 49 (October, 1964), p. 21.

among the Chinese and Japanese, whose over-all divorce rates were the lowest of any of major ethnic groups, "out-marriages of men with women of the other group may result in fewer divorces than the in-marriages in either group." [12]

BIOLOGICAL FUSION

The outcome of prevailing dispositions either to erase or to preserve existing ethnic lines in the next generation is perhaps most accurately, if not most dramatically, reflected in the record of the birth of children in Hawaii according to the ancestry of their parents. A summary of the nearly 200,000 births which occurred in Hawaii between July 1, 1931 and December 31, 1950 reveals a steady decline in the proportion of children whose ancestry was exclusively of one racial group—from 77.6 per cent during the first two years, to 69.5 per cent in the years 1938-1942, and to 66.7 per cent in the period of 1946-1950. A further study of nearly 83,000 births fifteen years later (1960-1964) revealed a further drop to 60.8 per cent in the pro-portion of "pure-blood" births.

All sixty-four of the possible racial combinations in births among the eight specified ethnic groups appear in both Tables 26 and 27, and the distribution in the number and types of racial mixtures indicate contributions from the various groups in much the same proportions as their marriages. The Hawaiians and Part-Hawaiians have obviously added the largest numbers to the population of mixed ancestry—some 46,570, or 76.1 per cent of all children of mixed ancestry born during the earlier twenty-year period. In proportion to their numbers, the smaller ethnic groups, such as the Koreans, Puerto Ricans, and even the Chinese, contributed more to the population of mixed ancestry than did the larger groups, but in absolute numbers the latter have added more. According to the data in Table 26, there were born 20,437 children of Part-Caucasian ancestry, of whom slightly more than half had also some Hawaiian blood. The next largest group of 10,721 births of mixed ancestry claimed Filipino ancestry on the side of either the father or the mother, while 9,033 claimed a Japanese parent, and only a slightly smaller number, 8,779, claimed a Chinese parent.

Among the notable new developments reflected in Table 27 is the fact that within the five-year period somewhat more than half as many children of mixed racial ancestry were born (32,492) as in the entire earlier twenty-year period (61,188). The proportion of the various

[12]*Ibid.*, p. 23.

26. BIRTHS BY RACE OF KNOWN PARENTS, JULY 1, 1931-DECEMBER 31, 1950*

FATHER	MOTHER									TOTAL	PER CENT MIXED
	Haw'n.	Part-Haw'n.	Cauca-sian	Chinese	Japanese	Korean	Filipino	Puerto Rican	All Others		
Hawaiian	4,374	3,704	422	205	190	32	38	46	26	9,037	51.6
Part-Hawaiian	3,126	14,329	2,364	1,364	1,238	261	429	166	109	23,386	100.0
Caucasian	1,631	6,910	32,784	926	2,543	579	823	905	229	47,330	30.7
Chinese	307	1,795	332	9,112	658	193	63	35	6	12,501	27.1
Japanese	282	1,282	475	435	66,134	192	74	32	6	68,912	4.0
Korean	79	256	97	134	280	1,535	25	13	4	2,423	36.6
Filipino	1,920	3,126	1,450	268	1,205	148	17,245	899	46	26,307	34.4
Puerto Rican	103	320	600	36	82	13	137	3,091	16	4,398	29.7
All Others	117	393	151	22	59	14	70	55	288	1,169	
TOTAL	11,939	32,115	38,675	12,502	72,389	2,967	18,904	5,242	730	195,463	
PER CENT MIXED	63.4	100.0	15.2	27.1	8.6	48.3	8.8	41.0			31.3

*Excluding the periods from July 1, 1933 to June 30, 1934 and from July 1, 1948 to December 31, 1948.

27. BIRTHS BY RACE OF KNOWN PARENTS, 1960-1964

Father	Mother										
	Haw'n.	Part-Haw'n.	Cauca-sian	Chinese	Japanese	Korean	Filipino	Puerto Rican	All Others	Total	Per Cent Mixed
Hawaiian	242	701	150	18	62	5	57	12	9	1,256	80.7
Part-Hawaiian	456	8,243	1,803	503	1,068	109	1,174	165	106	13,627	100.0
Caucasian	161	2,887	24,870	304	1,407	168	972	314	262	31,345	20.7
Chinese	23	475	223	2,128	694	49	106	13	13	3,724	42.9
Japanese	49	951	434	323	15,150	160	287	25	18	17,397	12.9
Korean	10	99	68	57	283	188	35	2	2	744	74.7
Filipino	162	2,167	656	130	582	49	6,521	181	202	10,650	38.8
Puerto Rican	35	393	174	16	63	7	126	548	10	1,371	60.0
All Others	30	354	191	16	68	7	88	27	1,237	2,877	42.4
TOTAL	1,167	18,246	28,569	3,495	19,377	742	9,366	1,287	2,718	82,991	
PER CENT MIXED	78.8	100.0	12.9	39.1	21.8	74.7	30.4	57.4	54.5		39.2

racial combinations had changed somewhat over the interval of time, with the children of Part-Hawaiian ancestry dropping from 76 per cent of all the mixed bloods to 69 per cent. Similarly the ratio of mixed-blood births with known Japanese ancestry increased from 14.7 per cent to 19.9 per cent, and of those with known Filipino ancestry there was an increase from 17.5 per cent to 23.3 per cent.

One of the most obvious conclusions to be derived from these two tables is that Hawaii's races are fusing at a rate that will make it increasingly difficult to distinguish between them in any meaningful fashion as time goes on. The smaller groups in particular are rapidly losing their separate identity. Thus of all children born during the twenty-year period with at least one Korean parent, 60 per cent had a non-Korean for the other parent, and by the later period this proportion had increased to 85.5 per cent. Slightly more than half (53.8 per cent) of all children born during the twenty-year period with at least one Puerto Rican parent had the other parent of non-Puerto Rican ancestry, and during the later five-year period this ratio had increased to 74.0 per cent.

Under the circumstances, it is not surprising that some observers of the Island scene should contend that the crossing of racial lines has already gone so far that it is useless and even misleading to compile any vital statistics by race. It must be recognized, on the other hand, that the majority of children born during these two periods presumably had both parents from a single ethnic stock and that their classification according to the usual racial categories would be accurate. Thus, in the earlier period 66,134 children were born with both parents pure Japanese, and they constituted 88.0 per cent of all the births with Japanese parents on either or both sides. By the later period, this ratio was still 82.4 per cent. In the case of children born of Caucasian ancestry, there were 32,874 with Caucasian parents on both sides in the earlier twenty-year period and 31,345 in the later five-year period, representing an increase in the proportion of "pure bloods" from 61.5 per cent to 70.9 per cent.

One is led to conclude that the biological fusion of Hawaii's people, although extensive and impressive as compared with most other areas of race and culture contacts, requires generations for its completion. It is reasonable to assume, and evidence from this and other sources support the proposition, that assimilation or the spiritual fusion of Hawaii's people moves more rapidly than amalgamation, but both processes are moving irresistibly forward. The peoples of Hawaii are becoming Hawaii's people.

INDEX